Financial Crises in Emerging Markets

Henry L. Stimson Lectures
Yale University

Financial Crises in Emerging Markets

An Essay on Financial Globalisation and Fragility

Alexandre Lamfalussy

Yale University Press   New Haven & London

Designed by Rebecca Gibb and set in Adobe Caslon type
by dix! Syracuse, New York.
Printed in the United States of America by Sheridan Books, Chelsea, Michigan.

Library of Congress Cataloguing-in-Publication Data
Lamfalussy, Alexandre.
Financial crises in emerging markets : an essay on financial globalisation
and fragility / Alexandre Lamfalussy.
p. cm.—(Henry L. Stimson lectures)
Includes index.
ISBN 0-300-08230-4
1. Business cycles. 2. Financial crises. I. Title.
II. Henry L. Stimson lectures, Yale University.

HB3711 .L24 2000
332—dc21   99-059157

A catalogue record for this book is available from the British Library.

The paper in this book meets the guidelines for permanence and durability of the Committee on Production Guidelines for Book Longevity of the Council on Library Resources.

10 9 8 7 6 5 4 3 2 1

For A. M.

Contents

Contents

Introduction

This book is about the potential impact of financial globalisation on financial fragility. I approach this broad topic from a specific angle, that is to say, by attempting to draw conclusions from a brief survey of four major crises that occurred in emerging markets: those of Latin America, 1982–83; Mexico, 1994–95; East Asia, 1997–98; and Russia, 1998. I do not deal explicitly with "homemade" crises (that is, domestic crises produced mainly by domestic factors) in the developed world, such as the 1987 stock market collapse in the United States or the Scandinavian banking crisis during the early 1990s.

The book has two origins: the first lies in my experience with both micro- and macroprudential issues while I was working with the Bank for International Settlements (BIS) from 1976 until the end of 1993. During these years I had the opportunity to observe from close quarters the development of bank supervisory and reg-

ulatory practices and the increasingly structured cooperation between national bank supervisory authorities as well as between
these authorities and supervisory agencies of other financial institutions and of financial markets. This was the microprudential aspect of my experience. At the same time I actively participated in
the endeavours of the central banks of the G-10 countries to minimise the risk that manifestations of fragility would assume systemic proportions—this is what we call in our bizarre jargon a
macroprudential concern.

It was in monitoring the explosive growth of international bank
lending during the second half of the 1970s that I began to realise
that the risk was not negligible. Although this first large-scale
manifestation of financial globalisation was bringing unquestionable benefits to the world economy, it was arguably also leading to
heightened instability. This concern, which I shared with most
G-10 central bankers, led to some practical results, the most visible
being the granting by the BIS of emergency "bridging loans" to the
central banks of crisis-stricken developing countries during the
first half of the 1980s. But it also led to substantial preventive efforts: the continued development of publicly available information on international bank lending; pioneering publications on
financial innovation in international banking; and not least, the
growing involvement of the G-10 central banks in the process of
improving the safety of international payment, clearing, and settlement systems, which were correctly identified as the key channels through which local crises could contaminate the global
financial system. I discussed, in the cautious style of central
bankers, much of this concern in the Annual Reports of the BIS as
well as in a number of speeches and conferences. However, as I

was approaching the date of my prospective retirement from the bank, I was beginning to entertain the idea of writing on my own behalf something lengthier on this topic: it would not be different in substance from what I was saying during my BIS years, but it could perhaps be said more bluntly. My appointment as president of the European Monetary Institute (EMI) at the end of 1993 led me to shelve this project. For three and half years I was busy preparing Stage III of Europe's Economic and Monetary Union: essentially, setting up the operational framework of the European Central Bank.

A couple of months after I relinquished my position as president of the EMI—at the end of June 1997—I accepted an invitation from Gustav Ranis, director of the Yale Center for International and Area Studies, to deliver the 1998 Henry L. Stimson Lectures. This gave me an opportunity to dust off my project. We agreed on the broad topic of globalisation and financial fragility; but with the obviously deepening East Asian crisis in mind, I decided to focus my lectures on emerging market crises. These lectures, delivered in March and April 1998, are the second origin of this book, which covers all the topics discussed in my lectures. In some respects I have even gone beyond them.

First, under the influence of the events of the summer of 1998, I included a short analysis of the Russian crisis, but I decided not to deal with Brazil: I had to stop somewhere. Second, and more important, I could not refrain from commenting on the strange global market reactions to this crisis. These reactions were remarkable in several respects. The initial severe decline of equity prices in developed countries, for example, seemed to be an overdue correction. The flight to quality also seemed a plausible reac-

tion. But what I could not understand—and still do not understand—was the extraordinary flight into liquidity in the U.S. debt
markets. A few weeks later I was surprised as much by the speedy
rebound of equity prices as by the fact that the "unusual strains" in
the U.S. debt and credit markets disappeared only after a noticeable time lag following the first two interest-rate cuts by the Federal Reserve Board and the reappearance of exuberance in the
equity markets. Finally, to compound my bewilderment, I noted
that the unpegging of the Brazilian real from the U.S. dollar in
January this year—an event that had been regarded only a couple
of months before as liable to produce a global financial meltdown—was in fact followed, after a short-lived shock, by manifestations of global financial euphoria. But will this euphoria be
borne out by subsequent developments?

What is the nature of this book? The only way I can answer this
question is by stating what I am *not* trying to do. This is not a history of the four specific crises mentioned above—at least, not in
any sense acceptable to professional historians—although my attempts at generalisation are underpinned by references to the historical experiences. It is even less an essay on the theory of financial
fragility, although I have kept in mind what I had learned as an un-
dergraduate in my classes on business-cycle theories as well as what
I have read more recently on information asymmetry, adverse selection, moral hazard, and the rationality of herd behaviour. It is
not a memoir either, although I draw on my professional experience with the BIS and in commercial banking before 1976; it was,
after all, during the first half of the 1970s that banks woke up to the
profit opportunities offered by globalisation. Finally, I explicitly re-

frain from presenting a blueprint for a "new financial architecture," although I do air my views on a number of issues relating to crisis prevention and crisis management.

This last point deserves some explanation. I would have had no reservation about offering such a blueprint if the expression "new financial architecture" were simply intended to cover proposals for greater transparency, the improved flow of information (or rather, the improved use of available information), the reformation of financial intermediation in emerging countries, or better supervision of institutions and markets—or better macroeconomic management in debtor countries and better macro policy management and coordination worldwide. I do in fact present my views on such courses of action in the last two chapters. But I have opted not to discuss issues related to a "new architecture" in two specific areas. One concerns crisis prevention and management techniques that have a strong legal and financial-engineering content. These are important issues which should be addressed by highly specialised working parties, not by an individual writer and not in this kind of book. The second, politically highly sensitive area is that of institutional reform. Should the institutions created by the 1944 U.N. Monetary and Financial Conference at Bretton Woods, N.H., particularly the International Monetary Fund (IMF), receive a new mandate? Should the decision-making procedures and operational techniques of the IMF be revised?

The easy and somewhat hypocritical excuse for not commenting on such issues would be that I do not possess adequate inside information and experience. But there is more to it. I doubt that the IMF should be held responsible for the severity of emerging market crises, as has become fashionable to argue nowadays. The

Fund *did* make mistakes in the field of crisis prevention and crisis management. But in many of these mistakes—bailing out the foreign holders of Tesobonos and letting the Russians sell rouble-denominated Treasury bills to foreigners are key examples—it had the strong support, to put it mildly, of its main shareholder. And the idea of writing into the Articles of Agreement of the IMF the full liberalisation of capital movements without specifying the preconditions was apparently supported by quite a few governments, officials, and academics (not to mention the business community)—and not only Americans. The insistence on fiscal surplus for the crisis-stricken Asian countries is perhaps the only major mistake which appears to have been produced directly and independently by the IMF staff. But who foresaw the severity of the contraction of Japan's domestic demand? Given the extraordinary challenges raised by financial globalisation, and given that we are navigating in waters uncharted by historical experience, I doubt that most of these mistakes could have been avoided by changing the IMF's decision-making procedures, by making these procedures more transparent, or by increasing the Fund's accountability vis-à-vis the shareholding governments. And I believe even less that reforming the institutional modus operandi of the IMF would play an instrumental role in keeping a tight rein on the propensity of our financial systems to periodically encourage excessive leverage, asset price bubbles, or the erosion of risk premiums. Focusing on such reforms could even provide a good excuse for not facing up to this very real problem.

A final remark concerning my sources. I relied to a large extent on BIS reports and on statistics collected or processed by the bank, for several reasons. For one thing I was familiar with them and knew their strengths and weaknesses. For another, I believe that, certainly in information on international banking but probably also in the broader field of financial intermediation and markets, the BIS possesses a comparative advantage over other multilateral institutions; and my focus was on these areas. Finally, I adopted a consistent approach in order to avoid the need to reconcile the (often not very significant) differences between statistics from various sources. I do not believe that using figures provided by other multilateral institutions would have altered my main generalisations.

In preparing this book I received substantial help from many quarters. I learned a lot from inquisitive questioning by Yale faculty and students after each of my Henry L. Stimson Lectures. More generally, I remain indebted to an army of central bankers, young and old, very junior or very senior, who taught me that it required optimism to believe that the conduct of a monetary policy geared to the stability of the consumer price index will necessarily ensure stability of the financial system. Such a policy will be helpful, but not in all circumstances. It is just as likely that reconciling these two policy objectives would require an unusual combination of professional skill, wisdom, imagination—and a measure of luck. In particular, thanks to Andrew Crockett's open mind and his keen interest in this topic. I learned a great deal from BIS economists who made valuable comments on my manuscript: Bill White, the economic adviser, Joseph Bisignano, Claudio Borio, Philip Turner, and many others. Wilhelm Fritz and his statisticians helped me with facts and figures, and the bank's translators corrected my often unreliable English. Finally, I am grateful for the hospitality and the logistical assistance extended to me by the Institut d'Etudes Européennes of the Université Catholique de Louvain, where I did most of my writing, and to Fabienne Wilmès who typed the manuscript.

Louvain-la-Neuve
April 1999

Chronology

Latin America, 1982–83

1973–82 Accelerating build up of large-scale external sovereign debt to the commercial banks of the developed countries.

1973 First oil shock.

1978–79 Second oil shock.

1979–82 Tightening of U.S. monetary policy accompanied by sharp increase in federal fiscal deficit.

1980–89 "Lost decade."

March 1982 First BIS bridging loan to Hungary, which is hit by the regionalisation syndrome produced by the Polish political crisis.

April 1982 The Falklands War.

August 1982 Outbreak of the Mexican crisis.

Autumn 1982–spring 1983 The external payments and debt crisis extends to most Latin American countries.

1982–83 Large-scale official liquidity assistance: IMF standby arrangements, often prefinanced by BIS and bilateral bridging loans.

1983–86 Debt rescheduling agreements.

1987–89 Debt restructuring and debt relief operations.

Mexico, 1994–95

1987 Beginning of structural reforms: trade liberalisation, deregulation, privatisation, fiscal reform.

1987–91 Deliberate use of exchange-rate policy as anti-inflationary device.

1991–early 1994 Large-scale capital inflows leading to the real appreciation of the peso; persistent large current account deficits.

March 1994 Assassination of the ruling party's presidential candidate. Reversal of capital flows.

March–December 1994 Accelerated issuance of Tesobonos and exchange-market intervention leading to the depletion of (net) foreign-exchange reserves.

December 1994 Enlargement of the exchange-rate fluctuation band, followed by floating of the peso, the collapse of the peso, and the collapse of the Mexican stock market.

Early 1995 IMF-led rescue operation amounting to $51.6 billion.

1995 Sharp recession, but recovery beginning in fourth quarter.

East Asia, 1997–98

Early 1980s–1996 East Asian "miracle," characterised by fast growth, high domestic saving ratios, and (with few exceptions) fiscal balance and single-digit inflation rates.

1990–96 Large-scale capital inflows leading to the accelerated build up of short-term external debt by the corporate sector and banks.

Early 1997 Pressure on the Thai baht signals turnaround in market sentiment. Heavy intervention by the Thai authorities.

July 1997 Floating and subsequently sharp depreciation of the baht. Market pressure spreads to the Indonesian, Malaysian, and Philippine currencies.

August 1997 IMF grants a $3.9 billion standby credit to Thailand.

October 1997 Pressure spreads to Korean won.

December 1998 Despite a $21 billion IMF standby credit, the Korean won starts floating.

1998 Deepening recession in all Asian countries hit by the crisis. However, from early spring, gradual stabilisation of the Thai and Korean currencies. Further depreciation of the Indonesian rupiah.

Late 1998–early 1999 Signs of recovery in Korea and Thailand; substantial recovery of stock markets in almost all crisis-stricken countries.

Spring 1999 Economic recovery confirmed, except in Indonesia.

Russia 1998

1993 Russia takes over Soviet foreign-currency debt.

1993–96 Despite sizeable current account surpluses, accumulation of additional external debt.

1996–97 Sharply rising capital outflows are offset by substantial capital inflows, which include large-scale foreign purchases of rouble-denominated government securities.

1997–98 Declining oil prices.

1998 Capital inflows dry up, while capital flight accelerates. With widening fiscal deficit, growing difficulties in financing the federal government's borrowing requirement. Steady pressure on the rouble.

Late spring 1998 IMF-led liquidity assistance for a total of $22.5 billion, usable by tranches.

August 1998 Russian government decides to unpeg the rouble (which plunges), suspends servicing its rouble-denominated debt, and prohibits banks from complying with their foreign-exchange commitments.

1998–early 1999 Continued capital flight, depreciating rouble, declining GDP; sharp rise in the rate of inflation (but no hyper-inflation).

Spring 1999 Industrial production is beginning to pick up; rising current account surplus.

Financial Crises in Emerging Markets

Four Crises in Emerging Markets

An Overview

A large number of developing countries—or, as we would now say, emerging markets—have been hit by financial crises since the early 1970s, with a sharply increased frequency since the early 1980s. I shall consider four major ones: those of Latin America, 1982–83; Mexico "Mark II," 1994–95; East Asia, 1997–98; and Russia, 1998. I have several reasons for my choices. One is that the size and nature of these crises raised concerns (and at the time of writing, the Asian and Russian crises still raise concerns) about their potential systemic implications, and the recognition of this led to large-scale rescue operations. At the same time, because of their origins and the way they unfolded, all four were part of the process of financial globalisation. In the end, however, despite their family resemblance they display striking differences. So striking, indeed, that they raise intriguing and disturbing questions about our ability to properly handle crisis situations. Shall we ever reach the point where we shall be able to identify the specificities of an emerging crisis from the outset? If not, how shall we be able to design the proper policy reactions? Even more disturbing, how can we foresee potential crisis situations and thus implement the correct prevention policies? Or to put it more bluntly: Is there genuine progress in our analytical ability to understand what is going on? The four crises considered here cannot be put on exactly the same footing. The first is firmly behind us, as is the second, although it has ramifications that still remain to be fully assessed. The Asian crisis seems to be under control, but not the Russian.

Latin America, 1982–83

The Latin American debt crisis erupted during the summer of 1982 in Mexico, spread to most of the Latin American countries during the following year, and affected a large number of other developing countries (but by no means all) as well. It led during the subsequent years to the rescheduling of the external bank debt of twenty-five developing countries, that is, of two-thirds of the outstanding bank debt of the whole of the developing world. At the risk of oversimplification, I would say that the debt crisis came about because the accumulation of foreign-currency-denominated sovereign banking debt had reached unsustainable levels. At the end of 1973 the non-OPEC developing countries carried a stock of net external foreign-currency bank debt of $4.5 billion.[1] By end-1982 the figure had reached $145.9 billion, an increase of $141.4 billion. During the same period, those countries accumulated current account deficits of around $336 billion, which meant that almost half of these deficits was "financed" by banks reporting to the BIS. This large-scale participation of commercial banks in capital flows to developing countries during the late 1970s and early 1980s can be regarded (together with similar flows, albeit on a smaller scale, towards Eastern Europe) as the first significant development of financial globalisation beyond the borders of the Organisation of Economic Cooperation and Development (OECD) world.

To understand how this truly spectacular development resulted in the 1982–83 crisis we need to make a chronological analysis, without which it would be exceedingly difficult to comprehend why "unsustainability" was recognised so late, but then so suddenly, by the lending banks, the borrowing governments, and, indeed, most Western governments, institutions, and officials. The following summary analysis is taken over in substance from the June 1983 Annual Report of the BIS, of which I was at that time editor.

The full period of debt build up (1974 to June 1982) can be divided into three distinct subperiods. The first—from late 1973 to early 1976—was dominated by the first oil shock. During the years 1970–73, the yearly current account deficit of non-OPEC developing countries averaged around $7 billion; it shot up to $21 billion in 1974 and to $31 billion in 1975. The resulting financing gap was covered to a large extent by loans from banks in the developed world, whose net claims on the borrowing countries jumped from a modest $4.5 billion at end-1973 to $25 billion by the end of 1975. The banks were able, indeed delighted, to lend. They experienced a massive inflow of funds from the OPEC countries at a time when, in a climate of recession, credit demand from their domestic borrowers dried up. They were helped by one of the first major (but by today's standards primitive) financial innovations, namely, variable-interest-rate or "rollover" loans, which were designed to protect the banks against adverse interest-rate developments on their short-term deposits—quite a high risk in an inflationary environment. This was the heyday of "recycling" the OPEC surplus, to the relief of the majority of Western officials. Nobody seems to have noticed at that time (a) that this marked the beginning of the crowding out, through unconditional bank lending, of conditional IMF and World Bank financing, and (b) that for the three large Latin American countries (Argentina, Brazil, and Mexico), the ratio of external bank debt to exports, which was around 100 percent at the end of 1973, increased to well over 200 percent by early 1976.

The second period, covering much of 1976 and 1977, contributed in no small way to maintaining the (almost) complete lack of concern about the new role being played by Western commercial banks in the financing of developing countries. During this period, many of these countries implemented domestic adjustment policies which, together with the recovery in the Western industrial world and the upswing in commodity prices, substantially reduced their current account deficits. Their net external banking exposure grew by only a little. The Latin American countries continued to borrow from Western banks, but much of this borrowing went into rebuilding their depleted foreign-exchange reserves. These developments confirmed, in the eyes of Western commercial banks, that the countries were respectable sovereign borrowers. At the same time, while the temporary disappearance of the OPEC surplus deprived the banks of additional OPEC funds, the large U.S. current account deficit combined with substantial capital exports from the United States provided the Western banking world with an ample supply of dollar-denominated liquidity. It is arguable that the relatively lax stance of U.S. monetary policy played a major role in this respect. It set the stage for a genuine borrowers' market for sovereign developing-country debt. Anyone who watched Western bankers queuing up outside the offices of officials of developing countries during the IMF–World Bank meetings received an almost physical impression of what a borrowers' market was.

The year 1978 marks the beginning of the third phase, which led straight to the 1982–83 crisis. During this period the growth of the net banking debt of the developing countries, in particular that of the three major Latin American countries, accelerated, rising from $36.5 billion at end-1977 to $146 billion by mid-1982. There were several factors at work, combining their influence to sustain this growth. The borrowers' market proved a temptation too strong to resist: the adjustment policies were abandoned, and the borrowing countries adopted expansionary fiscal and monetary policies. The second oil shock produced a sharp weakening in the countries' terms of trade, aggravated at a later stage by the decline of non-oil commodity prices. Mexico was in a special situation: it was about to become a major oil-exporting country and embarked on a sizeable spending programme in the expectation of future oil receipts. The slowdown of economic activity in the Western industrial world further aggravated the external position of the non-OPEC developing countries. The combined result was a drastic deterioration in the current accounts of developing countries—a deterioration, however, which was still relatively easily financed by borrowing from banks. One crucial factor took effect from 1980 onwards: the spectacular increase in short-term dollar interest rates, which reflected the sharp turnaround in U.S. monetary pol icy. Since a large part of the developing countries' external dollar debt took the form of rollover borrowings, the impact on the debt burden was almost instantaneous. For the three large Latin American debtors the ratio of net interest payments to exports, which fluctuated around 30 percent from 1975 until 1980, jumped to 50 percent by 1982. This meant that in 1982 almost the total of their large current account deficit ($23 billion) was accounted for by their net interest payments. For the non-OPEC developing countries as a whole, net interest payments represented three-quarters of their global current account deficit.

It was only a question of time before market participants would discover the "unsustainability" of the situation. Nationals of the countries involved were apparently well ahead of foreign lenders in hedging against a payments crisis. Although estimates of capital flight are notoriously untrustworthy, it is almost certain that private-sector capital outflows from the large Latin American countries during the years 1979–84 amounted to more than half their governments' net borrowings from abroad.[2] As is often the case with lenders (or investors), they recognized the true situation only after a major "external" shock—the Falklands War—although the radical shortening of the maturity profile of Mexico's external debt had already started in 1980.

Domestic policy mismanagement in the borrowing countries and external events beyond their control each played a role in the development of major current account deficits, which were the basis of the eventually unsustainable accumulation of external debt. To ascribe the responsibility to either of these two influences alone would seem a hopeless exercise. Their respective roles varied over time; moreover, the margin of manoeuvre of domestic policies was in some cases severely constrained by external developments—such as swings in commodity prices or interest rates. That being said, table 1.1 shows clearly (despite reservations about such back-of-the envelope simulations) that although the recession in the industrial world, terms-of-trade developments, and the high dollar-denominated interest rates did have a dramatic impact on the balance of payments of the non-OPEC developing countries, the rate at which imports by (and therefore domestic demand in) these countries grew between 1977 and 1980 would have been unsustainable, even in less unfavourable external circumstances.

Table 1.1   Non-OPEC Developing Countries: Actual and Hypothetical Current Account Balances, 1980–82 (in billions of U.S. dollars)

Items	Trade balance			Net services and transfers			Current account			Estimated gross (external debt)		
	1980	1981	1982	1980	1981	1982	1980	1981	1982	1980	1981	1982
Actual	−56	−61	−43	−9	−18	−24	−65	−79	−67	380	450	500
Hypothetical												
Scenario I[a]	−56	−48	−7	−7	−10	−12	−63	−58	−19	380	430	440
Scenario II[b]	−56	−62	−65	−7	−11	−16	−63	−73	−81	380	460	520

[a] Scenario I assumes constant terms of trade in 1981 and 1982; an increase in export volumes in 1982 in line with the 1977–81 average increase of 7 percent; an average interest rate on foreign debt in 1980–82 of 7.2 percent; the actual average interest rate of 1979; and imports at the level actually recorded.

[b] Scenario II assumes that the volume of imports rose in 1981 and 1982 in the line with the 1977–80 average growth of 7 percent, but maintains the other assumptions made in Scenario I.

Source: BIS Annual Report, June 1983, p. 91.

Fig. 1 Features of External Banking Indebtedness of Selected
Countries, 1978–82

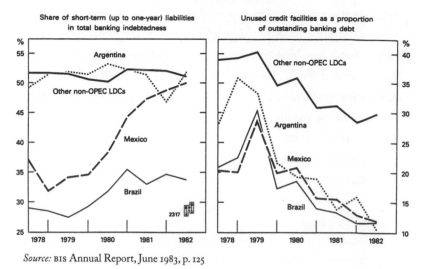

Source: BIS Annual Report, June 1983, p. 125

We should exercise caution when passing judgement on the banks' enthusiastic participation in the process of "overborrowing" (or, from their angle, "overlending") and on their very late recognition of unsustainability. The banks' initial role in recycling the OPEC surpluses was almost universally applauded; they were not alone in believing that sovereign borrowers cannot go bankrupt or that the major Latin American countries had been endowed with natural resources (Mexico and Venezuela had large oil reserves, for example) which made them relatively safe debtors. It would have been asking a lot of the banks, in terms of forecasting ability, to foresee the violent external shock suffered by developing countries as a result of the combined influence of the Western recession, high short-term interest rates, and the strong dollar. On one key point, however, the banks have no excuse. Several years before the outbreak of the crisis, they could see from the BIS international banking statistics that the external debt of major borrowers was rising at an exceptionally fast pace and that by any standards the figures were becoming enormous. These data also revealed the short maturity profile of the debt, as well as the sharp decline of unused credit facilities from 1979 onwards (see figures 1 and 2).

What about the attitude of Western officials? As I said above, the role of commercial banks in the recycling process after the first oil shock was applauded by most officials; a number also publicly encouraged commercial bank lending after the second, 1979, oil shock, although by that time the adjustment-versus-financing debate was beginning to gather momentum. Officials in West Germany, who had already voiced their concern about excessive financing in 1973, became more vocal by that time and gained the support of other officials in OECD discussions.

I am in no position to reveal what debate—if any—went on behind the scenes between governments or inside the IMF or the World Bank. But a few facts concerning the attitude of central banks are worth recording. It is instructive to contrast the tone of two BIS Annual Reports. Here is a key passage from the conclusion to the June 1978 report:

A remark about the flow of aid and long-term capital to developing countries. For these countries . . . moderate current account deficits are a normal feature of the international pattern of trade and payments. What is less normal is that the deficits in question should be covered increasingly by medium-term bank loans, often at variable interest rates. Fi-

Fig. 2 Evolution of Gross and Net Banking Indebtedness of Selected Countries, 1975–82 (in billions of U.S. dollars)

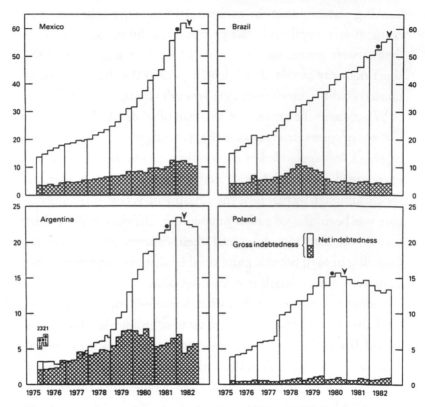

Note: Arrows at the top of the columns show the quarters in which financial problems arose; dots indicate the latest figures on banking debt available at that time. The graphs include valuation changes resulting from exchange-rate movements but not positions vis-à-vis banks in Switzerland. Despite these imperfections, the graphs demonstrate clearly that in all four cases it was possible to observe a strong build up of debt over a number of years before the outbreak of the external-payments crises.

Source: BIS Annual Report, June 1983, p. 127.

nancing of this kind involves high and unpredictable annual debt service charges for the countries concerned and renders the lending banks themselves increasingly vulnerable to country risks. As a general rule, the greater part of the financing should consist of aid, long-term loans and direct investment. (p. 157)

The Annual Report published in June 1982 on the eve of the Mexican crisis struck a different note. By this time the lesson to be drawn from the Polish debt crisis, and its extension to the rest of Eastern Europe, was well understood, and it became obvious that the Falklands War could trigger a similar "regionalisation syndrome." Hence the report's insistence that banks should not withdraw abruptly and indiscriminately from the financing of developing countries (see Appendix A).

The 1978 report signalled the increasing concern of central bank governors about the growing involvement of banks in the financing of current account deficits by Western banks. The same concern could also be detected in the comments of the BIS when it published its quarterly and half-yearly statistics on international bank lending. From 1978–79 onwards the BIS began to refer explicitly to the external bank-debt accumulation of major Latin American debtor countries. Naming countries was not an easy decision to take: the action could in itself precipitate a crisis. It was only after some hesitation, therefore, that the reporting central banks accepted this innovation. Finally, the G-10 governors published a press communiqué in April 1980 (see Appendix B) which, while couched in very prudent terms, expressed their concern.

But these examples reflect only the publicly visible part of the governors' endeavour. As an obvious borrowers' market developed from 1976 onwards, the question arose in discussion among the G-10 group of central banks as to whether it would be possible to rein in the proclivity of banks towards manifest overlending. The "moral-hazard" argument ruled out from the outset establishing an officially endorsed country risk-rating system, and even more, direct intervention of bank supervisory organisations in the lending decisions of banks. The chairman of the Federal Reserve Board, Arthur Burns, suggested working out a set of questions for banks to ask sovereign borrowers before taking their lending decision. This "checklist" would comprise information on countries' balance of payments, domestic macroeconomic indicators, external reserves position, external debt, and so forth. Banks would commit themselves to obtaining this information prior to lending but would draw their own conclusions from it and remain free to take their own lending decision.

The G-10 governors entrusted me, in my capacity as economic adviser of the BIS, with the task of exploring the willingness of the major international banks to enter voluntarily into such an arrangement. I did this, with the assistance of Michael Dealtry and in co-operation with the central banks concerned, during the summer of 1977. Fifty-seven banks were approached at that time. I failed to secure their support. Some banks found the idea attractive, but the majority were either sceptical about the feasibility of the project or openly hostile. A few of them (mostly the very large ones) argued explicitly that they did not need central bankers to teach them how to assess sovereign credit risks: they had been in that business, quite successfully, for some time. Most of them simply feared that not all the banks would respect the checklist procedure, and the virtuous ones would lose lucrative business to their unfair competitors. The G-10 governors continued to discuss the situation and eventually published, rather late, their April 1980 press communiqué. To cut a long story short, central bank endeavours to slow the sharp rise in unconditional international bank lending failed. So did the crisis prevention warnings of the June 1982 BIS Annual Report.

The sharp increase in the burden of net interest payments during the years 1980–82 played a significant role in precipitating the debtor countries towards an external-payments crisis. As I mentioned above, the banks adopted the rollover pricing technique for their medium-term loans in order to protect themselves against the risk of an unpredictable increase in short-term rates on their liabilities. This was—or seemed to be—a prudent hedging device for all banks, but even more for the nondollar-based banks. The hedging device worked: the banks' interest margins were protected. But what the banks gained in this respect was lost (and probably more than lost) in terms of credit risk, by raising the borrowers' debt burden to intolerable levels. This was akin to a situation in which a shrewd customer would have managed to extort from his insurer an exceptionally favourable insurance policy—so favourable, indeed that the materialisation of a very large risk pushed the insurance company into bankruptcy. This is an experience worth keeping in mind in the current world of spreading derivative hedging devices.

Although the first signs of external payments difficulties appeared during the second quarter of 1982 in Argentina, the really violent crisis broke out in Mexico during the first days of August, then spread to Brazil and finally, through the regionalisation syndrome, to most of Latin America. The proximate cause of the payments crisis was a combination of the sharp acceleration of capital flight with the sudden turnaround in the attitude of lending banks, which refused to renew expiring short-term claims. A reminder: by mid-1982 claims maturing within one year amounted to around 50 percent of Mexico's and Argentina's external bank debt, and 34 percent of that of Brazil.

Western officials immediately realised that a unilateral suspension of debt-service payments, let alone a formal moratorium, could have systemic effects by threatening the stability of the Western banking system. The exposure of the nine largest U.S. banks to Latin American countries as a group—claims on Latin America as a percentage of their equity—was at that time more than 170 percent, and some European and Japanese banks also had ratios that substantially exceeded 100 percent. The firefighting initiatives of Western central banks, governments, and the IMF were correspondingly swift, efficient, and successful, in contrast to their inability to prevent the emergence of the crisis.

The first step consisted of granting emergency credits to the central banks of the debtor countries. These credits were very large by the standards of that time. The U.S. monetary authorities and the BIS, in association with its member central banks, were in the forefront of this action. In early August, the Bank of Mexico drew on its swap facility with the Federal Reserve Bank of New York for an amount of $700 million and the U.S. government paid $1 billion in advance for future oil delivery; on 30 August the Bank of Mexico received a bridging loan of $1,850 million in anticipation of a drawing on the enlarged IMF facility. Half of this loan was granted by the BIS, the other half by the U.S. monetary authorities. In January 1983 the BIS granted a $500 million facility to Argentina and a month later $1,450 million to Brazil.

The second step, closely tied to the first, involved the speedy granting of large IMF facilities: $3.8 billion to Mexico, $2.2 billion to Argentina, $5.4 billion to Brazil. These loans were designed to be conditional in two respects. First, the borrowing countries had to undertake domestic adjustment policies. Second, the loans were linked to receiving new facilities by the banks—this condition is what allowed the managing director of the Fund, Jacques de Larosière, to say quite rightly that the banks were in fact bailed "in" rather than bailed "out." Given the size and the maturity profile of bank claims and the fact that the importance of interest payments made it practically impossible to achieve current account balance, continued bank lending was an essential part of the rescue packages.

The third stage started in 1983 and went on for several years. Initially it involved the medium-term rescheduling of short-term bank debt. But from 1985–86 onwards the emphasis began to shift towards debt-management negotiations which implied, in the end, increasing elements of debt relief. An analysis of these techniques goes beyond the scope of this book.

The crisis management was indubitably successful in one major respect: it prevented the Latin American payments crisis from developing into a full-blown international financial crisis with unpredictable "real" consequences for the world economy as a whole. Given the size of bank exposure to Latin America such a scenario was a genuine risk, although as with other systemic risks it is impossible to quantify it, even with hindsight.

The crisis management can also be regarded as successful in another sense. The fact that the sovereign debtors did not declare a unilateral moratorium and, even more important, did not renege on their debt obligations gave the banks enough time to restore their own health. Debtor countries also agreed to enter into negotiations with the banks, often under the explicit guidance, or at least the watchful eyes, of the IMF. These negotiations were complex, pro-tracted, and often acrimonious. But the rescheduling and, at a later stage, the debt-relief agreements allowed the world trading and fi-nancial system to remain reasonably open, and therefore paved the way for the later, substantial expansion of world trade and private capital flows. Admittedly, the possibility that the negotiations would be successful was enhanced by the nature of the problem: sovereign debtors facing an identifiable number of lending banks. This was a very different world from the one we live in today.

There is, however, a third respect in which the success of crisis management has been questioned. It is often argued that the ad-justment process imposed on the debtor countries was too radical. By forcing the debtor countries to undertake, as of 1983, an out-ward real resource transfer on a very large scale,[3] and by achieving this through expenditure cutting rather than expenditure switch-ing, the debt-management strategy produced massive unemploy-ment and unnecessary hardship for those debtor countries—a lost decade for Latin America. Growth would have been resumed, and the debt-GDP ratio brought under better control much earlier, so runs the argument, if the financing-adjustment mix had been more heavily weighted in favour of financing than adjustment.

I have two reasons for not sharing this conclusion. First, sub-stantially more financing—private or public—was just not avail-able. The second, more judgemental, reason is that the leeway granted to the governments by a gentler adjustment process would not necessarily have led to domestic policies that restored conditions for growth. A higher probability could be assigned to the opposite outcome: continued large-scale domestic capital flight and less, rather than more, investment. In the short run, private consumption might have held up, but the end result would have been even more uncontrollable domestic chaos.

Mexico, 1994–95

There is one striking—and quite real—similarity between the Latin American experiences in 1982–83 and the 1994–95 Mexican crisis. Both were preceded by large-scale and persistent current account deficits (see table 1.2). There is also another, but potentially misleading similarity: private capital inflows not only adequately "financed" the current account deficits until 1994 but, with the additional help of official capital inflows, even allowed the build up of external reserves. During the period 1990–93, Mexico's net external reserve position improved by $18 billion (table 1.3). But the sequence of events and the chain of causality establishing the accounting identities in the balance of payments were quite different.

Table 1.2   Mexico: Current Account Balance

Balance as a percentage of	1990	1991	1992	1993	1994	1995
Gross Domestic Product	−3.0	−5.0	−7.3	−5.8	−7.0	−0.6
Exports of goods and nonfactor services	−15.3	−28.4	−44.1	−38.1	−41.7	−1.8

Sources: IMF balance of payments statistics and IMF international financial statistics.

Table 1.3   Mexico: Balance of Payments
(in billions of U.S. dollars)

	1990	1991	1992	1993	1994	1995
Current account balance	−7.4	−14.6	−24.4	−23.4	−29.7	−1.6
Net private capital inflows	5.8	19.9	23.5	30.2	10.3	−13.3
Net official capital inflows	5.0	2.4	2.0	−0.9	0.9	24.5
Net change in external reserve position	3.4	7.7	1.0	5.9	−18.4	9.6

Note: Capital flows are calculated as the difference between the current account and the change in reserves; private flows are calculated as a residual from an estimate of official flows.

Sources: IMF balance of payments statistics and Institute of International Finance (IIF).

There can be little doubt that the major driving force behind (what turned out to be) an unsustainable accumulation of current account deficits was private capital inflows. During the four-year period 1990–93 about half of these inflows ($36 billion) took the form of portfolio investments. The role of banks was significant ($22.2 billion), but they did not dominate the scene as they had done before the 1982–83 crisis. Foreign direct investment also played its part ($16.2 billion; see table 1.4). These capital inflows were attracted by the climate and the results of economic reforms set in motion during the late 1980s. Deregulation and privatisation, the elimination of fiscal deficits, positive real interest rates, and steadily declining inflation all played their part. A sizeable portion of portfolio investments found its way into common stocks. By the end of 1993 equity prices expressed in U.S. dollars had reached a level which was ten times as high as that of the 1985–89 average—a

Table 1.4   Mexico: Main Components of Private Capital Inflows
(in billions of U.S. dollars)

	1990	1991	1992	1993	1994	1995
Foreign direct investment	2.6	4.8	4.4	4.4	11.0	9.5
Portfolio						
Equity	2.0	6.3	4.8	10.7	4.1	0.5
Bonds	1.1	1.3	3.6	6.3	2.8	−0.5
Banks	9.1	7.9	1.6	3.6	−0.3	−4.3
Memorandum item: Tesobonos[a]	NA	0.6	0.7	2.0	30.1	0.3

[a] Total stocks of Tesobonos at end of period.

Sources: IMF balance of payments statistics and national data.

rate of increase that vastly outstripped the performance of other emerging markets. Contrary to what had occurred fifteen years previously, there was no deliberate government borrowing during these years to finance current account deficits.

These large-scale capital inflows maintained the nominal value of the Mexican currency vis-à-vis the U.S. dollar, with the result that the real effective exchange rate steadily appreciated from 1990 onwards: by the end of 1993 it had gained more than 30 percent in comparison with 1990. It is possible that the peso had been undervalued to some extent at the beginning of the decade, yet a real appreciation of this speed and size was bound to have an effect on the current account. But it is arguable that capital inflows played an additional, though perhaps indirect, role in allowing the current account to deteriorate. It did so because sterilisation was not complete. Thus the monetary base expanded at a rate higher than would have been required for maintaining domestic monetary bal-

Table 1.5   Mexico: Credit and Money Supply Developments
(annual percentage changes)

	1990	1991	1992	1993	1994	1995
Bank credit	26.5	29.9	26.6	13.5	34.9	31.8
Monetary aggregates						
Central bank money	35.3	27.8	14.4	10.4	21.2	33.4
Broad money (M2)	46.2	47.2	20.4	14.4	22.7	35.6

Source: IMF international financial statistics.

ance, allowing the banking system to undertake a fast pace of credit expansion to the private sector (table 1.5). Liberalisation gave the banks the necessary freedom to make this expansion; the reduction of government borrowing provided them with a stimulus; and after many years of limited access to bank credit by corporations and households, there was a genuine demand for banking reintermediation. Initially this helped maintain gross capital formation, but from 1990 to 1992 it also led to a dramatic decline in the private saving ratio: from 14.3 percent to 9.6 percent. The national saving ratio fell to less than 15 percent by 1994, from an average of more than 20 percent in the second half of the 1980s (table 1.6). To make matters worse, by trying to achieve as much sterilisation as possible the Mexican monetary authorities kept the peso interest rate relatively high—not high enough to discourage excessive domestic borrowing in pesos but high enough to encourage borrowing by corporations in dollars.

The relation between the current account deficit and capital inflows changed dramatically in early spring 1994. Throughout January and February, spontaneous portfolio capital inflows still

Table 1.6   Mexico: Current Account Balance and Domestic Counterparts
(as a percentage of Gross Domestic Product)

	1990	1991	1992	1993	1994	1995
Gross fixed capital formation	17.9	18.6	19.6	18.6	19.4	16.2
Change in inventories	5.3	4.7	3.7	2.4	2.4	3.7
Financing of gross capital formation	23.2	23.3	23.3	21.0	21.8	19.9
Current account balance	−2.8	−4.7	−6.7	−5.9	−6.9	−0.5
Gross domestic saving	20.4	18.6	16.6	15.2	14.7	19.4
Public sector	6.1	8.5	7.0	5.1	4.4	4.8
Private sector	14.3	10.1	9.6	10.1	10.4	14.6

Note: Foreign saving is equal to the current account balance.

Source: National Accounts of Mexico (INEGI).

dominated the scene—so much so that the Mexican monetary authorities were increasingly confronted with the unenviable task of trying to reconcile the unreconcilable: preventing the peso from appreciating and at the same time sterilising the domestic monetary impact of the inflow. From March 1994 onwards, however, spontaneous capital flows dried up, and this began to exert downward pressure on the exchange rate. The proximate cause was the assassination of the PRI's presidential candidate, an action which raised doubts about the political stability of the country. The Mexican authorities reacted by countering the potential depletion of foreign-exchange reserves with the issuance of Tesobonos: dollar-indexed Treasury bills—of which foreign investors held $17 billion at end-December 1994. This was genuine, government-induced foreign borrowing on an unprecedented scale, much different from the earlier portfolio capital inflows. At the same time, domestic purchasers also bought Tesobonos on a large scale. As a result, foreign-exchange reserves net of Tesobonos became negative from July onwards. The visible crisis began in the last months of 1994, with an accelerating capital flight that could no longer be "financed" by the further issuance of Tesobonos and led therefore to the spectacular depletion of gross foreign-exchange reserves. By December it had become clear that the exchange rate could no longer be supported, and the Mexican authorities decided to let it float. Its collapse was accompanied by that of the Mexican stock exchange.

Just as in 1982, this second Mexican crisis spread to other countries. Net spontaneous private capital flows to other Latin American countries dried up, and some of the currencies, notably that of Brazil, came under pressure. But this "tequila effect" did not last long.

Mexico Mark II differed fundamentally from the 1982–83 crisis in that the blame could not be put to any significant extent on the mismanagement of domestic macroeconomic policy. By 1993 the rate of inflation had dropped below 10 percent and, even more important, the budget deficit was well under control. Even if we discount onetime privatisation receipts from public-sector revenue, it would be difficult to argue that the large current account deficit found its counterpart in public-sector profligacy. Rather, it appeared in the private sector's saving and investment imbalances— more specifically, in the decline and low level of the saving ratio.

Yet the current account deficit turned out to be unsustainable, to a large extent because the size and nature of the capital inflows which helped to bring it about and in the last stage financed it created a degree of fragility which exposed the country to external shocks. The external shock was in this case political uncertainty created by the assassination of the presidential candidate and the Chiapas uprising. One culprit in this process was exchange-rate pegging—responsible (to some extent) for the emergence of the current account deficit and for the explosive growth of foreign currency debt (both of corporations and, in 1994, in Tesobonos).

Also responsible for the deficit unsustainability is the fact that the process of deregulation and liberalisation was not matched by an adequate strengthening of domestic financial intermediation. Yearly expansion of bank credit to domestic corporations and households at a rate of 20 to 30 percent would have put any banking system under stress. But what could be expected from banks whose lending activities had previously been tightly controlled and which simultaneously experienced the quasi-disappearance of their traditional borrower—the government—and an explosive demand for credit by the private sector? This was not simply a matter of inefficient banking surveillance. What Mexican banks needed was a well-functioning internal risk-assessment and control mechanism, and it is absurd to believe that such a mechanism could have been achieved without a long learning period, in particular in a macroeconomic environment that was undergoing radical change.

As with the international banks' imprudent overlending before the 1982 crisis, portfolio investors and banks during the years 1990–93 and, to a lesser extent, foreign purchasers of Tesobonos in 1994 did have some excuses for their behaviour. The radical structural reforms undertaken by Mexico, in particular financial deregulation, capital flow liberalisation, and privatisation, were received with almost universal enthusiasm. Just as important, the restoration of fiscal discipline accompanied by an apparently successful process of disinflation earned the country a great deal of praise. Mexico was viewed as a model for other Latin American countries. Nor is it easy to find an explicit warning by Western governments or multilateral institutions concerning the unsustainability of Mexico's large current account deficit. There was some expression of concern by Western central banks in BIS meetings, but these concerns filtered into the June 1993 BIS Annual Report only in the form of a brief reference to the high degree of volatility of portfolio investment (p. 110). Finally, it is worth recalling that one of the prevailing academic fads was the argument that current account deficits mattered only to the extent that they mirrored a public-sector deficit. This view was not shared by all economists, not even by most politicians, but it did receive a lot of media attention.

Nonetheless, investors cannot argue that they were deprived of information during the period of spontaneous capital inflows. The size of Mexico's current account deficit was known; so was the fact of large-scale portfolio capital inflows. It was also recognized that the saving ratio of the private sector had declined to very low levels. Finally, the equity market's exuberance, as well its volatility, was no secret either—nor was the spectacular expansion of domestic bank credit. Admittedly, information on the dramatic decline of foreign-exchange reserves (net of borrowing Tesobonos) was not given by the authorities, but data on Tesobonos issuance were available, though not instantaneously. Nobody was prevented from comparing the level of gross reserves with the outstanding Tesobonos debt.

Although it would be hard to avoid reservations about the pre-crisis management by the Mexican authorities between March and December 1994—in particular over the Tesobonos episode—

there can be little doubt that after the outbreak of the "visible" crisis in December 1994 both domestic and international policy action was swift and determined, and it can be regarded, in the short run at least, as successful.

The domestic action consisted of the abandonment of exchange-rate pegging, coupled with a sharp jump in short-term interest rates (which exceeded 70 percent in March 1995) and a tight fiscal policy. The international manoeuvre depended on official foreign assistance on an unprecedented scale. The total amount came to $51.6 billion (of which, however, the BIS–G-10 commitment of $10 billion was not activated). The IMF provided $17.8 billion, bilateral commitments reached $21 billion, and the contribution of the International Bank for Reconstruction and Development (IBRD) and the Asian Development Bank (ADB) totalled $2.8 billion. This made it possible to cover substantial capital outflows, including the redemption of more than $16 billion in Tesobonos held by foreigners, and permitted the partial replenishment of the country's depleted foreign-exchange reserves.

The combined effects of these measures were spectacular. Initially, there was a sharp recession with a steep decline in real wages, large-scale unemployment, and a drop of more than 10 percent in industrial production. After a few hiccups, however, the peso stabilised, the initially sharp rise in inflation abated, and the trade balance swung into surplus. Industrial production started rising from the late summer of 1995 onwards, and by late 1996 exceeded the precrisis peak.

My concern about the long-term effects of the crisis management in Mexico has two aspects. First, it is not yet clear (in the spring of 1999) how the Mexican banking system and domestic corporations have managed to digest the impact of the sharp rise in interest rates and of the recession. We know that the cost of rescuing the Mexican banks may reach $65 billion; but we do not know the precise amount and manner of the burden sharing. Second, and perhaps more important from a global standpoint, the large-scale external assistance, which in practice amounted to the massive bailout of foreign Tesobonos holders, may well have had moral-hazard implications for the future. It is true that foreign holders of Mexican equities suffered sharp losses; but holders of Tesobonos did not lose a penny.

East Asia, 1997–98

The origin and nature of the crisis are clear, but its outcome, both for the countries directly concerned and in its wider implications are uncertain—despite the recovery which started in early 1999. Moreover, understanding through hindsight does not mean that the violence and depth of the crisis was foreseeable—in fact, I could not find any publicly available explicit warning, either by private forecasters or by official institutions, that the financial meltdown experienced by Indonesia, Thailand, and Korea was imminent. And for good reason, too. All these countries enjoyed throughout the late 1980s and the 1990s exceptionally high saving and investment ratios, strong growth, fiscal balance, subdued inflation, and—in the case of Korea and Indonesia (but not Thailand)—relatively modest current account deficits (table 1.7). This was a situation completely different from that of the Latin American countries before 1982–83 and, although to a somewhat lesser extent, from that of Mexico in the early 1990s.

Table 1.7   Macroeconomic Structure of Selected Asian Economies
(as a percentage of Gross Domestic Product)

	Investment		Domestic saving		Fiscal balance[a]		Openness to trade[b]		ICOR[c]	
	Average 1986–95	1996	Average 1986–95	1996	Average 1986–95	1996	1986	1996	Average 1986–95	Average 1991–96
Indonesia	32.6	31.2	33.8	31.2	0.9	−1.0	15.9	20.4	19.2	22.6
Korea	33.9	36.8	36.4	35.2	0.3	0.0	30.7	28.9	32.9	20.2
Malaysia	32.7	42.2	35.8	42.6	−3.2	0.7	44.3	78.9	25.1	22.1
Philippines	20.5	23.2	17.5	15.6	−1.9	0.3	16.4	31.2	20.5	12.2
Thailand	36.3	42.2	33.5	35.9	2.1	0.7	20.9	34.9	32.6	19.6

[a] Central government.

[b] Ratio of average merchandise exports and imports to GDP.

[c] Incremental capital-output ratio, shown here as its inverse, i.e., the real rate of GDP growth over investment-GDP ratio.

Source: BIS Annual Report, June 1998, p. 35.

As I shall argue, however, some of the ingredients of the earlier Latin American and Mexican experiences could be detected by anyone who cared to look at the available information. During the years 1990–96, for example, Thailand had an average current account deficit of close to 7 percent of GDP. In addition, all these countries were engaged in building up a large external foreign-currency debt to banks—moreover, a debt with an exceptionally short maturity profile; domestic bank credit was expanding at a high rate; and there were clear indications that financial and real estate bubbles were developing. How did this combination of apparently great strength with some visible weaknesses become an explosive mix?

As has been pointed out forcefully by the BIS Annual Report of June 1998 (pp. 35–36), one of the major features of the "real" economic background to the crisis is the process of "overinvestment" which led to substantial excess capacities in such key industries as electronics, automobile production, household appliances, and, most important, real estate investment. This should not come as a surprise to anyone who is at all familiar with traditional business-cycle theories. Average real rates of growth of 6–8 percent, which characterised the three countries for more than fifteen years, will breed a climate of extrapolative exuberance which is almost bound to result in an excessive accumulation of real capital. As is shown in the BIS Annual Report the growth rate of GDP relative to the investment-GDP ratio (that is, the inverse of the incremental capital-output ratio) declined sharply during the first half of the 1990s. In Thailand it fell from 32.9 to 20.2; in Korea from 32.9 to 20.2; and in the Philippines from 20.5 to 12.2. However crude this measure may be, a fall of this size signals a radical deterioration in profitability—or, to put it differently, an increasing vulnerability to shocks, be they "real" or financial, internal or external.

This vulnerability was considerably increased by the way domestic capital accumulation was financed. Reliable comprehensive statistics on sources and uses of funds by the enterprise sector are not available, but data on both domestic and international banking intermediation and on other international capital inflows allow us to paint a reasonably coherent picture of what went wrong.

As regards domestic financial intermediation, the most visible feature was the consistently fast growth of bank credit to the private sector. For the period 1981–97 the average annual rate of expansion in real terms was 13 percent in Korea, 17 percent in

Thailand, and 25 percent in Indonesia. These spectacular figures mean that corporations relied essentially on bank credit for financing, and that at the same time the corporate sector's leverage was bound to increase. That this happened at a time of relatively high short-term interest rates shows how deeply rooted was the expectation—in both borrowers and lenders—that real growth would go on indefinitely at the rate experienced during the previous fifteen years. It also shows how risky it is to undertake financial-sector liberalisation at a time when everything seems to be going well. Before liberalisation, banks managed to keep their profit margins up thanks to interest ceilings on deposits and the lack of genuine competition on the lending side. Liberalisation resulted in pressure on profit margins, but in a world of seemingly riskless permanent growth, banks responded by reckless expansion rather than cost cutting.

The situation was materially aggravated by foreign-currency lending by international banks to both domestic banks and domestic nonbanks. Table 1.8 shows the size and chronology of both flows, as well as of net bond issuance and net equity inflows. We can see the spectacular growth of corporate leverage denominated in foreign currency during the years 1995–96, as well as the even more impressive growth of foreign-currency-denominated debt by the domestic banking sector. About two-thirds of this interbank debt had a maturity of less than one year. The counterpart to this large-scale, very short-term interbank borrowing in foreign currency was medium-to-long-term claims in domestic currency on domestic corporations. As we now know, neither the maturity transformation nor the currency risk was hedged by the domestic banks at the beginning—as a matter of fact, frantic attempts at

Table 1.8   International Bank and Bond Finance for Five Asian Countries
(in billions of U.S. dollars, annual rates for the period 1990–1997
Q 3, actual rates for 1997 Q 4)

	1990–94	1995 Q1–1996 Q3	1996 Q4–1997 Q3	1997 Q4
Net interbank lending	14	43	11	−31
Bank lending to nonbanks	2	15	˙ 11	−1
Net bond issuance	3	17	32	1
Total	19	75	54	−31
Memorandum item	1990–94	1995–96	1997	
Net equity inflows[a]	11	17	2	

Note: The countries are Indonesia, Korea, Malaysia, the Philippines, and Thailand.

[a] IIF estimates of direct investment and portfolio equity flows.

Sources: IIF and BIS.

hedging in the early stages of the currency crisis bear a major responsibility for the depletion of foreign-exchange reserves. Part of the domestic claims were secured by real estate mortgages but at margins which gave no protection when the asset-price bubble collapsed.

There is little doubt that the pegging of the East Asian currencies to the U.S. dollar played a significant role in the foregoing developments. It certainly blunted market participants' awareness of a potential foreign-exchange risk—although I find it difficult to understand what appears to have been not just diminished awareness but its complete absence. Pegging also made things more difficult for the local monetary authorities. When signs of overheating were beginning to appear—real estate bubbles and the deterioration of some of the current accounts—the authorities were hindered by the strong capital inflows from raising domestic interest rates sufficiently. Finally, and perhaps most important, pegging to the dollar exposed these countries to the unpredictable, and in some cases damaging, gyration of the dollar against the yen and the European currencies. Given the countries' export and import structures and the location of their competitors, this was a major risk—a much bigger one than was implied by the dollar-pegging of the Latin American currencies. The period of dollar weakness allowed the East Asian countries to maintain and even to increase their competitiveness despite having higher inflation than the United States; but with the strengthening of the dollar[4] their real effective exchange rates rose sharply during 1996 and 1997.

Although the exchange-rate regime was an important channel for external influences, there were two other external factors at work which also played a part in precipitating the crisis. As mentioned above, one such factor was the easy availability of foreign-currency bank credit. That lending banks neglected some of the warning signals and accepted risks rather late in the day seems to me beyond question.[5] But in addition to sharing the general optimism (or myopia) about the underlying strength of the "Tigers," the banks have an additional excuse: globally liquid money markets in 1995 and 1996. Under the combined influence of a fast reduction of U.S. short-term rates in 1995 (which followed a short-lived tightening in 1994), the continued easing of European rates in the presence of the steady reduction of inflation, and a sluggish economy, real broad money growth in the developed world picked up significantly from mid-1995 onwards. The second

31

external influence was the rather sudden turnaround in Japan's economic situation. The Japanese economy expanded at a relatively satisfactory pace until the first quarter of 1997, but under the impact of the April fiscal package the growth of domestic demand stalled, then during the second half of the year, declined. This played an important role not so much in triggering the Thai crisis as in spreading it to other countries.

The crisis started in Thailand when foreign lenders and investors suddenly took note of the country's large current account deficit—more than 8 percent of GDP in 1996—and its disappointing export performance, which they attributed to the deterioration of its competitive position. The baht appeared to be overvalued. With real estate overcapacity becoming evident and with the decline in equity prices, short-term capital started moving out at a fast pace. The initial outflow seems to have been generated by equity investors and by the efforts of domestic banks and corporations to hedge their foreign-currency exposure. The central bank lost its net reserves within a few months, and the authorities were forced to let the baht float in early July. It was from June onwards that foreign bank lending turned into a massive outflow: during the second half of 1997 banks reduced their claims on Thailand by close to $18 billion.[6]

The Thai crisis triggered a regionalisation syndrome akin to the one produced by the 1982–83 crisis and the "tequila" contagion in 1994–95. It spread to Indonesia and affected Malaysia and, to a smaller extent, the Philippines. Korea was drawn into the turmoil at a relatively early stage, when the slowing of its economy during the summer of 1997 exposed the fragility of its highly geared corporations. The size and violence of the crisis can be best assessed by the turnaround of net private capital flows (which include not only bank lending but also securities issues and portfolio investment). The main Asian capital-importing countries,[7] China excluded, attracted from 1991 to 1996 net private capital inflows for a cumulative total of $235 billion, that is, at an average annual rate of $39 billion; the actual figure peaked at $77 billion in 1996. In the first half of 1997 there was still a substantial inflow—$31 billion—followed in the second half of the same year by an outflow of $54 billion.

The crisis management has generated fierce controversy—understandably so, given the novel aspects of the crisis. The controversy is centred to a large extent on the issues of the desirable mix of monetary and fiscal policy and of the exchange-rate regime or policy. There is little discussion about the need to significantly improve the process of domestic financial intermediation in general, and the working of the banking system in particular. Nor is there much doubt (except perhaps in the minds of hard-liners in the U.S. House of Representatives) about the need to provide official liquidity assistance to the crisis-stricken countries: the prospect of a generalised unilateral debt moratorium is not appealing. Official liquidity assistance to Asia does, however, raise a few difficult issues. In the following I venture to make a few remarks of my own, dealing first with official liquidity assistance, then with issues relating to domestic financial intermediation, and finally with the policy mix and the exchange-rate regime or policy.

Official liquidity assistance to Thailand, Indonesia, and Korea was swift and large scale (table 1.9). The IMF provided financing commitments totalling $35 billion, the IBRD $16.4 billion, and the ADB $9.7 billion. In addition, bilateral commitments added up to

33

$56.1 billion. The grand total came to $117.1 billion, more than double the figure given to Mexico in 1994–95. But this much larger figure was insufficient to cover the three countries' maturing short-term obligations, whereas the smaller had been enough for Mexico, hence the initially dubious market reaction when the packages were announced. But there is another difference between the Asian situation and the Mexican. In the case of the Asian countries there is nothing comparable to the Tesobonos held by foreign investors. The maturing Asian obligations are external debt obligations of banks or corporations owed to private foreign lenders or investors. Since the evident purpose of foreign official assistance to the three countries' governments is to allow at least the partial repayment of privately owed external debt to private lenders and investors, these lenders and investors were effectively bailed out by their own governments. Admittedly, this also happened in the case of Mexico—but there it was at least arguable that the creditworthiness of the Mexican government was directly at stake.

Putting the matter in this (oversimplified) form raises at the same time frightening moral-hazard implications as well as the prospect of nationalising (or renationalising) domestic banks and corporations. To contain the moral-hazard risk would have required the kind of bailing-in approach to private lenders that was pursued, with success, after the 1982–83 crisis. The involvement of a much larger number of banks and the role of securities financing, and of securitisation in general, made it far more difficult to enter into formal rescheduling agreements. Nevertheless, some rescheduling or rollover agreements were made at a later stage and appeared to have been quite useful.

34

Table 1.9 Official Financing Commitments
(in billions of U.S. dollars)

	1982–83			Mexico 1995	Asia			Russia
	Mexico	Brazil	Argentina		Thailand	Indonesia	Korea	
BIS–G-10	1.850	1.450	0.5	(10.0)*				
IMF	3.8	5.4	2.2	17.8	3.9	10.1	21	
Bilateral commitments	2.7			21.0	12.1	22.0	22	
IBRD				1.5	1.9	4.5	10	
ADB				1.3	2.2	3.5	4	
Total				51.6	20.1	40.0	57.0	22.5

* Not activated.

Source: BIS Annual Report 1998, p. 134.

The question of how to deal with the domestic banks or corporations' sharply increasing debt to their governments or central banks leads us to the broader topic of the reformation of the systems of domestic financial intermediation. In light of what was said about the reckless growth of bank lending before the crisis, I have no doubt that such reformation needs to be undertaken. To improve the risk-assessment and risk-control techniques of any banking system is a long-term business under any circumstances. When one adds the task of clearing up the mess created by weak corporate governance and incestuous links between industry and government, the reform process becomes extremely difficult. And when all this has to be carried out with what are in effect bankrupt banks, the task appears to become overwhelming. Consider, moreover, the fact that the combination of the (unavoidable) unwinding of a lengthy process of excess investment with a recession exacerbated by an exchange-rate crisis has led to such weakness of the corporate sector that the value of the banks' claims on this sector can be assessed, if at all, only by guesswork.

This leads us to the most controversial issue raised by crisis management in Asia: the exchange-rate policy and the macroeconomic policy mix implemented as the central piece of crisis management.

There was no practical alternative, so it seems to me, to the unpegging of the currencies. Given (a) the maturity profile of the external debt, (b) the unavailability of additional funds from international organisations or foreign governments, and (c) the major practical difficulties in organising, within a matter of weeks, standstill agreements with foreign lenders and investors, the floating of these currencies became unavoidable. But it could be legitimately feared that the resulting depreciation would go well beyond what would have been required to reestablish external balance; "overshootings" in such cases are the rule rather than the exception. This would have implied the reactivation of inflation and inflationary expectations and, even more important, the wholesale bankruptcy of corporations and banks that were overburdened by high leverage and unhedged foreign-currency debt exposure.

To insist, therefore, that as part of the rescue packages these countries immediately tighten their domestic monetary policy appeared to be the lesser evil. Such a condition implied, of course, that domestic corporations had to face a significant additional burden from the increase in domestic interest rates; but one could hope that monetary tightening would eventually lead to the stabilisation of the external value of the currencies.

As of the beginning of 1999 we know that these expectations have been fulfilled, although after a longer than hoped-for time lag in the cases of Korea and Thailand. Interest rates shot up to very high levels in both countries and the exchange rate collapsed during the first months of the crisis. The maximum depreciation against the U.S. dollar (in January 1998) was about 55 percent for both countries. From that point onwards, the exchange rates began to strengthen and since the summer of 1998 have tended to stabilise at a depreciation level of 25 percent against the U.S. dollar in both countries, whereas in nominal effective terms Korea showed a depreciation of 30 percent and Thailand one of 14 percent. In real effective terms, Korea suffered a depreciation of 25 percent and Thailand of 7 percent. By that time, domestic short-term interest rates had fallen below 10 percent. Indonesia's situation is much less encouraging. In early 1999 depreciation amounted to 33 percent against the U.S. dollar, and 67 percent in nominal effective terms (40 percent in real effective terms), while short-term interest rates were still 40 percent. In addition, the rate of inflation has risen significantly, whereas it has been kept under control in Thailand and Korea.

On balance it seems to me arguable that the IMF's monetary policy prescription was the right one. On the other hand, its fiscal policy recommendation—demanding, for instance a fiscal surplus for Thailand—was not. It was based, I believe, on the need to engineer a current account turnaround, which has indeed been achieved—but by cutting imports rather than by stimulating exports. Exports to the United States and to Europe increased, but exports to Japan declined dramatically. As was acknowledged by Michel Camdessus, the managing director of the IMF, the Fund's policy prescription was based on the expectation that the Japanese economy would not stumble into recession. Although the IMF has by now accepted the relaxation of fiscal policy, the damage has been done: the East Asian countries' deep recession—a drop of more than 10 percent of GDP by end-1998—has been aggravated. By how much is anybody's guess.

Russia, 1998

The Russian crisis broke out in August 1998 when the authorities decided to unpeg the rouble, declared a unilateral moratorium on their rouble-denominated internal (and some external) debt, and prohibited banks from complying with their foreign-exchange commitments.

Russia's crisis bears two strong resemblances to the three other crisis episodes: it had been preceded by the build up of a large external debt; and the economy had operated under a system of pegged exchange rates. For the rest, although there are some resemblances in other areas—for instance, a high public-sector deficit—some of these are superficial rather than real, and the differences between the crises are substantial. Most significant, the crisis revealed (even to those who had preferred not to notice it before) Russia's basic domestic institutional and structural weaknesses: a government that was unable to devise, let alone implement, a coherent economic policy; a public administration that was unable to administer; a regulatory framework which either did not exist or was not enforced; and the almost complete absence of some of the legal and institutional foundations (such as well-defined property rights, a clear system of taxation, and a bankruptcy law) without which no market economy can function.

There are no comprehensive and reliable data on Russia's external assets and liabilities position. Some of the available, fragmented information is provided from external sources. As can be seen from table 1.10, the total sum of Russia's identifiable external liabilities at the end of 1997 stood at $128 billion. Identified Russian assets totalled $27.7 billion, of which foreign-exchange reserves amounted to $13 billion, one-tenth of the liabilities. Even more significant, these reserves were less than the foreign holdings of short-term rouble-denominated Treasury bills. It was quite clear at that time that Russia's capacity to service its external debt depended crucially on the confidence of foreign lenders and investors in the country's willingness and ability to secure IMF assistance and, therefore, to comply with IMF conditions—the key demand being adequate tax collection and the reduction of the federal government's deficit. I shall say more about this below.

Table 1.10   Russia: External Assets and Liabilities Position
(in billions of U.S. dollars, at end of period)

	1992	1993	1994	1995	1996	1997	1998
Russian Claims							
Foreign-exchange reserves	2.0	5.8	4.0	14.4	11.3	13.0	8.2[a]
BIS banks' liabilities to Russia	—	9.4	10.3	11.6	15.6	14.7	14.6[b]
Russian liabilities							
BIS banks' claims on Russia	—	47.2	47.7	49.5	53.6	58.8	64.1
Official claims (IMF, World Bank, etc.)	1.7	3.5	5.4	11.4	15.3	18.7	—
Foreign holdings of rouble-denominated T-bills					6.3	16.1	—
Foreign holdings of foreign-currency-denominated Russian bonds, *of which*					2.0[c]	35.0	—
Securitised ex-Soviet debt (London Club)						28.0	—

[a] August.

[b] June.

[c] Partly estimated.

Sources: National data and IMF.

Perhaps even more important, domestic confidence also had to be secured—a matter that Western lenders and investors tended to overlook. Yet the IMF had been publishing data on Russia's balance of payments for years (see table 1.11). In every year from 1994 to 1997 Russia ran very large trade surpluses and comfortable current account surpluses. At the same time, the country enjoyed capital inflows: modest amounts of foreign direct investment ($11.3 billion for the whole period), continued IMF assistance ($11.7 billion) and, especially in 1996 and 1997, substantial portfolio investments

($56.3 billion). How is it, then, that Russia's foreign-exchange reserves increased from end-1993 to end-1997 by only $7.2 billion? The answer is that there were substantial capital outflows. During the two years when Western confidence in Russia turned into euphoria (1996 and especially 1997), capital outflows amounted to

Table 1.11   Russia: Balance of Payments
(in billions of U.S. dollars)

	1994	1995	1996	1997
Merchandise exports	67.8	82.7	90.6	88.9
Merchandise imports	50.0	61.9	67.5	71.3
Trade balance	17.8	20.8	23.1	17.6
Services and transfers, net	−8.5	−12.9	−11.0	−14.3
Current balance	9.3	7.9	12.1	3.3
Direct investment in Russia	0.6	2.0	2.5	6.2
Portfolio investment in Russia, *of which*	−0.1	0.1	9.9	46.4
Equity securities	0	0.1	2.2	2.5
Debt securities	−0.1	0	7.7	43.9
Other investment in Russia, *of which*	−13.6	−16.9	−6.3	−2.9
General government	−14.4	−12.5	−12.1	−17.3
Banks	1.3	2.4	4.2	8.4
Other sectors	−0.5	−6.8	1.5	6.1
IMF credit and loans	1.5	5.5	3.2	1.5
Exceptional financing	18.2	16.0	16.1	−15.9
Other capital inflows	5.5	3.1	3.1	2.1
Total capital inflows	12.2	9.8	28.5	37.5
Capital outflows	−23.0	0.5	−35.3	−31.7
Capital balance	−10.8	10.3	−6.8	5.7
Errors and omissions	−0.4	−7.9	−8.1	−7.2
Overall balance = change in reserve assets	−1.9	10.4	−2.8	1.9

Source: IMF

$67 billion, which was about equivalent to the total sum of capital inflows ($66 billion). This was an extraordinary manifestation of asymmetrical expectations: exuberance on one side, deep mistrust on the other. At first sight it would seem impossible to argue that both were rational. Yet perhaps they were. Foreign investors were attracted by exceptional profit opportunities and hoped to be bailed out. Domestic owners of capital could not entertain such a hope and did not believe that the stability of the rouble would last. Note, however, the silver lining implied by these capital outflows. Over time Russians acquired a large amount of external assets: from end-1993 to end-1997, these amounted to close to $100 billion. We know next to nothing about how these assets are held. Domestically held cash is reported (or assumed) to be sizeable; so are real estate and financial investments abroad. In any event, Russia's external assets and liabilities position is much stronger than would appear from table 1.11, but for this potential strength to become actual, Russians must be induced to invest at home in rouble-denominated assets. Capital flows activated by Russians are as much part of the problem as they could be part of the solution.

It was because of the crucial importance of preserving or establishing confidence that (as far as I could tell from my position on the outside) the IMF insisted so strongly on the implementation of policies leading to domestic price stability and the reduction of the large, persistent federal deficit. I think the Fund was right in its identification of the problems, but it probably underestimated (along with many others) the underlying structural and institutional weaknesses of Russia which made it impossible to achieve this double objective fast enough—or at least in a sustainable manner.

Table 1.12   Russia: Price and Exchange-Rate Developments
(end of period year-on-year percentage change)

	1992	1993	1994	1995	1996	1997	July 98	Sept. 98
Consumer price inflation	2,528.8	839.8	214.7	131.4	21.8	11.0	5.5	67.6
U.S. dollar appreciation against the rouble	145.3	200.5	184.7	30.7	19.8	7.2	8.0	173.6

Sources: National data and IMF.

Price stability was supposed to be achieved, and preserved, by the implementation of a tough monetary policy, supported by the pegging of the rouble to the U.S. dollar. As shown in table 1.12, the rate of inflation, which at end-1993 was 840 percent, declined to 131 percent by end-1995, and then sharply decelerated, to reach its lowest level in July 1998 (5.5 percent). Price stability was in sight— or so it seemed. But several ominous developments accompanied this process of stabilisation. The monetary tightening took place in an environment in which no orderly bankruptcy procedures existed, thereby eliminating the possibility of genuine industrial restructuring. Restructuring was made even more unlikely as a result of a phoney privatisation process, which did not allow radical changes in management. Tight money therefore led to the huge increase of the barter system and, even worse, to mounting wage arrears. The tight money policy was accompanied, at the same time, by high nominal and real short-term interest rates. In late 1997, interest rates on rouble-denominated Treasury bills fluctuated between 20 percent and 45 percent. At that time, the rate of inflation was down to 11 percent. Such interest rates did not do much harm to the majority of corporations, which borrowed little from banks; but they made it impossible for those corporations to even consider borrowing in future. The banks, on the other hand, accumulated Treasury bills in their portfolios and earned exceptionally high margins. The most ominous sign, however, was that capital outflows went on unabated. Russians may have been proud of the rouble's newly acquired stability (as was reported by Western media), but they did not act that way.

At the same time, no real improvement occurred in the reduction of the fiscal deficit (table 1.13). Tax collection by the federal government, which was still close to 15 percent of GDP in 1993, fell to 10.2 percent in January 1998. Although the deficit did decline to 4.5 percent of GDP, this happened because federal expenditures also fell, from 20.7 percent of GDP to 14.7 percent. This was not the result of a well-thought-out, deliberate policy of expenditure reduction. The federal government simply delayed paying wages, pensions, and suppliers of goods and services.

None of the developments noted above were secret; nor did they accelerate dramatically during the months preceding the crisis. What, then, happened during the first half of 1998 that led to

Table 1.13   Russia's Federal Budget
(as a percentage of Gross Domestic Product)

	1992	1993	1994	1995	1996	1997	Jan. 98
Revenue		14.9	14.2	12.7	11.5	12.0	10.2
Expenditure		20.7	24.0	18.1	19.4	19.1	14.7
Balance		−5.8	−9.8	−5.4	−7.9	−7.1	−4.5

Sources: National data.

the August crisis? The single most important external event was that the weakness of oil prices, which had already been visible in 1997, turned into a sharp decline. In January 1998 Brent in London was still close to $17; in August it fell below $12. Given Russia's massive reliance on exports of oil and natural gas for its foreign-exchange receipts, the deterioration of the current account, and even the appearance of a deficit, became a distinct possibility. By early summer it had become evident that the major Western countries were unwilling to increase the IMF-led rescue package of $22.6 billion enough to assure the market that the Russian authorities had adequate financing to continue servicing their external debt. The IMF itself was getting visibly worried about the willingness or ability of the Russian authorities to comply with its conditions for releasing further tranches of its package. Capital outflows accelerated sharply in July, and in August the Russian authorities decided to let the rouble plunge and declared a unilateral moratorium on servicing their internal debt.

In the weeks following the August measures the rouble did, indeed, plunge; so did equity prices and the value of Russian government bonds. The majority of Russian banks became bankrupt. In October inflation started accelerating and economic activity declining. With the collapse of tax receipts and the prospect of the liberal use of money printing there was a genuine danger that the price increases would escalate into hyperinflation and that the country would move into a deep and lasting recession.

This disaster scenario has not materialised. By early 1999 the rate of inflation reached three digits, but its acceleration had come to a halt. Industrial production first stopped declining, then started growing. The trade balance moved again into surplus.

What happened? The sharp depreciation of the rouble did its job: it put a brake on imports and gave a boost to industrial production. Hyperinflation was prevented by moderation in the use of the printing press. Most important, perhaps, the upturn of oil prices make it possible that the regained trade surplus will prove sustainable.

There are no signs, however, of any improvement in "structural" fundamentals. No reforms have been initiated to tackle Russia's basic institutional weaknesses. Capital exports seem to have continued at the rate permitted by the improvement in the current account—and possibly beyond.

2

Four Crises in Emerging Markets

Specificities and Common Features

The four crises reviewed in the preceding chapter display a bewildering variety. Here I shall try to sort out their common features from the maze of specific factors which apparently dominated each of these major episodes. To help the reader, and to support my own analytical discipline, I have constructed a synoptic table that compares the key features of these crises under five headings: balance-of-payments and exchange market developments before the crisis, domestic developments before the crisis, the development of the crisis, contagion, and crisis management (table 2.1). Any such synthesis is, of course, bound to suffer from oversimplification. But if used with caution, the table will help the reader identify the common features of the four crises.

Table 2.1 Synopses of the Four Market Crises

	Latin America, 1982–83	Mexico, 1994–95	East Asia, 1997–98	Russia, 1998
Balance of payments and exchange-rate developments before the crisis				
Capital inflows	Substantial	Substantial	Substantial	Substantial
Who were the foreign lenders or investors?	Banks	Investment funds; institutional investors; corporations (FDI); banks	Banks; investment funds; institutional investors; corporations (FDI)	Banks; investment funds; institutional investors
Who were the domestic borrowers or users of funds?	Government or other public authorities	Corporations; banks; in final stage, government	Corporations; banks	Government; banks, stock purchases in markets and privatisation
What were the vehicles of capital inflows?	Rollover loans (mostly syndicated)	Bonds; equity; Treasury bills; FDI	Interbank deposits; loans; bonds; equity; FDI	Treasury bills and bonds; interbank deposits; bonds; equity
Capital outflows	Substantial and persistent	Moderate until early 1994, then substantial	None until few months before the crisis, then strong	Very substantial and persistent
Current account	Large-scale deficits	Large-scale deficits	Significant deficits for Thailand, smaller ones for Korea, Malaysia, and the Philippines	Surplus, but at end of period moving towards deficit

Exchange-rate regime and developments	Pegging	Pegging; real appreciation	Pegging; real appreciation	Pegging, real appreciation
Regulatory framework	Exchange control	Freedom	Freedom	Freedom
External macro policy (and other) influences	Major movements in U.S. interest rates and terms of trade; oil shocks	High international liquidity	Highly liquid international banks; movements in dollar-yen exchange rate; Japanese stagnation	Towards end of period: oil and commodity price declines
Domestic developments before the crisis				
Macro policies	Lax fiscal and monetary policies	Apparently conservative fiscal and monetary policies	Conservative fiscal policies; apparently conservative monetary policies	Unmanageable fiscal deficit; first inflationary then restrictive monetary policy
Saving-investment balance and growth rate	High public-sector deficits	Low private-sector saving ratio, growth picking up	Very fast growth; high saving ratio, even higher investment ratio	First GDP decline, stabilisation in 1997
Domestic credit expansion	Fast	Fast	Fast	(No significant domestic credit)

Table 2.1 Synopses of the Four Market Crises (*cont.*)

	Latin America, 1982–83	Mexico, 1994–95	East Asia, 1997–98	Russia, 1998
Domestic price level	Inflation	Declining inflation rate	Low inflation	After hyperinflation, strongly declining inflation rate
Equity and real asset price developments	Underdevelopment	Boom	Boom, but reaching peak before outbreak of crisis	Boom, but reaching peak before outbreak of crisis
Regulatory framework for domestic financial system	Strong regulation	Liberalisation and deregulation in full swing	Liberalisation and deregulation in full swing	No genuine financial intermediation; anarchical liberalisation
Crisis developments				
Role of external or internal "shocks" triggering the crisis	Falklands War	Assassination of presidential candidate; Chiapas	None	Oil price decline; political crisis and unilateral moratorium
External influences aggravating the crisis	None	None	Japanese recession	Continued oil-price weakness
Domestic capital flight	Continued	Substantial	Massive hedging attempts by banks	Accelerating
Flight by foreign lenders and investors	Substantial	Substantial	Substantial	Substantial

Contagion

Where from?	Eastern Europe	No source	Thailand	Asia
Where to?	All Latin American countries, plus other developing countries	Other Latin American countries: "tequila effect"	Other Southeast and East Asian countries	Latin America (Brazil) and financial markets in developed countries

Crisis management

Size of the IMF–led rescue packages	Mexico, Brazil, Argentina: $17.9 billion total	Mexico: $51.6 billion	Thailand, Indonesia, Korea: $117 billion total	Russia: $22.5 billion
Macro policy conditionality	Strong	Strong	Strong	Strong, but dismal record of enforcing
Micro policy conditionality	None	Strong	Strong	Strong, but dismal record of enforcing
Private sector contribution to crisis handling: bailing in or bailing out	Bailing in	Bailing out	Initially bailing out; soon after, bailing in	Unilateral moratorium and rescheduling

Specific Factors

Balance-of-Payments and Exchange Market Developments

In all four instances, there were large-scale, persistent capital in-flows into the countries concerned, leading to the build up of an eventually unsustainable external-debt position. There were, how-ever, a great diversity of lenders and investors, a variety of vehicles, and a number of domestic users.

Among the lenders, banks dominated the scene in Latin Amer-ica, played a significant role both in Asia and in Russia, and had a more modest part in Mexico. Their participation predominantly took the form of adjustable interest-rate or rollover contracts (of short- or medium-term maturity), interbank deposits, and, in the case of Russia, purchases of Treasury bills. A variety of institutional investors—mostly mutual funds—were the main investors in Mex-ico Mark II and also played an important role, along with banks, in Asia and Russia. They bought both equity participations and fixed-income paper, both short and medium-to-long term. There was also direct investment by foreign corporations, especially in Asia. On the side of domestic users, sovereign borrowers represented al-most 100 percent of the total in Latin America, played a last-minute but crucial (in fact, devastating) role in Mexico (the Tesobonos episode) and were important both in the initial build up of the (Soviet) debt and during the later period, when Russia sold Treasury bills to foreigners. Most bank claims were denominated in foreign currency, as were the medium- and long-term bonds sold to foreign investors. This was also in practice true of Tesobonos but not of the Russian Treasury bills bought by foreigners.

The balance-of-payments counterparts—in the national accounting sense—of these capital inflows also varied greatly, and this variety becomes quite bewildering when one tries to uncover the chain of causality hiding behind national accounting identities. In Latin America, sovereign external bank borrowing was used deliberately to finance large current account deficits and, on occasion, to rebuild official foreign-exchange reserves, but it also covered—willy-nilly—large private capital outflows. In the case of Mexico, the dominant accounting counterpart was increasing current account deficits, though arguably with a reversed chain of causality. Private capital exports also played a role, a massive one, when doubts emerged about the sustainability of pegging. In Asia, current account deficits remained relatively modest, with the notable exception of Thailand, and this led to the build up of foreign-exchange reserves. There do not seem to have been capital outflows until the five to six months preceding the visible outbreak of the crisis (in the case of Thailand, the floating of the baht in early July 1997), but as a result of last-minute hedging plus genuinely speculative positions taken in the expectation of currency depreciation, these outflows became sizeable. In the case of Russia, foreign-exchange borrowing was undertaken during the Soviet years to cover current account deficits. However, already at that stage (and more significantly later on), when the current account registered surpluses capital inflows "financed" large-scale outflows of domestic capital.

Setting aside for a moment the domestic developments which can be regarded as having played their part either in the build up of external debt or in making this debt unsustainable (see below), the next lines in the synoptic table signal the role of some external factors. One such factor—whether to call it external or internal is a moot point—is the exchange rate, coupled with changes in the regulation of capital flows. Pegging the exchange rate to the U.S. dollar turned out to be a pretty explosive device for both Mexico and the Asian countries. The move played a similar role in the case of Russia. External macro policy influences were very active in the Latin American and East Asian crises. Negative real dollar interest rates, followed by the shift of U.S. monetary policy towards tightening, played a significant role in Latin America. The high degree of banking liquidity during the early 1990s, coupled with the weakness of the dollar in 1994–96, contributed significantly to the overheating of the Asian economies—just as the strengthening of the dollar from 1996 onwards combined with Japanese stagnation to exert a depressive influence on the same countries.

Finally, a reminder about the regulatory framework. This framework was asymmetrical in the case of Latin America: the lending banks were operating in a fairly liberal environment, with no administrative (and only mild prudential) constraints on their international lending activities, while, on the receiving end, controls on balance-of-payments operations were the rule. But this did not prevent sovereign borrowers from borrowing in foreign currency. The framework became far more symmetrical in the subsequent crises, with huge steps towards liberalisation in Mexico and Asia regarding capital account transactions on the balance of payments, and with a high degree of freedom—basically anarchical—in Russia.

Domestic developments

According to the now prevailing conventional wisdom there is a stark, fundamental contrast between the 1982–83 crisis on the one hand and the Mexican and Asian crises on the other, with Russia falling into a category of its own, albeit with some similarity to 1982–83 Latin America. Global macroeconomic mismanagement (fiscal laxity and inflation) characterised Latin America in the late 1970s and early 1980s. The "twin deficit" argument clearly applied to these countries: domestic fiscal imbalances played a major role in sustaining large current account deficits. By contrast, there were no fiscal deficits in Mexico and in the Asian countries, and "responsible" monetary policies were keeping inflation under control. As we saw in the previous chapter, this contrast is, broadly speaking, valid, but it should be qualified, and we should note differences both between Mexico and Asia and among Asian countries.

One common feature of Mexico and Asia is that, to the extent that there was a significant current account deficit, its counterpart was to be found in a domestic *private* saving-investment imbalance. But while in the Mexican case this meant a low and initially sharply declining private saving ratio, in Asia it implied very high saving ratios and on occasion even higher investment ratios. A common feature to both was reckless credit expansion, which does not fit into the picture of "responsible" monetary policy. We learnt in the previous chapter that capital account liberalisation coupled with exchange-rate pegging goes a long way towards explaining the monetary authorities' inability to maintain appropriate monetary tightness. But it should also be observed that although bank credit growth did not create a major inflationary upsurge (as measured by the CPI), it certainly contributed to the explosion of real estate prices and to the bull market in equities.

The credit explosion, in turn, cannot be attributed exclusively to the (understandable) failures of monetary policy. In both cases, deregulation of domestic financial intermediation, greater competition, lack of managerial experience, weak or inadequately enforced prudential standards, and incestuous industry banking relationships played a key role. Nor should we forget, in the case of Asia, the influence exerted by persistently high real growth rates on the perception of risk by the managements of both corporations and financial intermediaries—or on foreign lenders and investors.

The Russian case falls into a special category from almost all angles. A sizeable part of Russia's external debt was inherited from the Soviet Union. As for the additional debt accumulation by Russia, its balance-of-payments counterpart was to a large extent capital exports. Russia ran current account surpluses which led to the build up of foreign-exchange reserves and were large enough to allow capital exports in excess of capital imports. Domestically, external borrowing both in foreign currency and in rouble-denominated Treasury bills and bonds served to cover part of the federal government's gaping fiscal deficit, which itself was caused by the failure of tax collection.

Common Features or Discernible Trends?

The Build Up of an Unsustainable External Debt Burden

All the crises had been preceded by a fast or persistent, but always large-scale, build up of external debt which eventually became unsustainable in the eyes of external or domestic market participants. The debt was either denominated in foreign currencies—mostly in dollars, often in yen, sometimes in deutsche marks or other European currencies—or its repayment would have implied in some other way that the debtor country would draw on its foreign-exchange reserves or put pressure on its exchange rate. The nature and composition of capital inflows varied from case to case or over time, but these inflows always comprised, either from the beginning of the debt build up or in its more advanced stages, a substantial proportion of claims that were maturing within a short period. Interbank deposits, short-term rollover loans, or purchases of Treasury bills are prime examples. And even when capital inflows were not debt creating in the precise sense of the term, that is, when they took the form of equity purchases, a notable part of these purchases were portfolio investments carried out by institutions accustomed to actively managing their portfolios (rather than holding securities in a long-term perspective). Direct investment, while not negligible (especially in Asia), in no case constituted the bulk of capital inflows.

Common Features (or Their Absence) in Debt Accumulation

If I am right in singling out excessive foreign debt accumulation as the most striking common feature of the four crisis experiences, the question arises as to what similarities can be detected in the process of debt accumulation. The first, not very original observation is that excessive debt accumulation could not have taken place without the demand for funds meeting the supply, or vice versa. There could not have been "overborrowing" without "overlending." But which of the two—supply or demand—was the driving force behind the process of debt accumulation varied from case to case, and even over time within the same episode. In some instances it is just not possible to allocate primary responsibility to one or the other side. Who can say that apparently demand-led "overborrowing" was not initiated, or at least encouraged, by the lenders? After all, roadshows by potential issuers of debt have often been organised, or facilitated, by financial intermediaries—mainly Western investment banks—which have a stake in finding opportunities for lenders to lend and investors to invest. Moreover, there have been numerous instances when the leading role of supply appears in the price indicators: eroding risk premiums or upward pressure on the exchange rate of capital-importing countries.

It would be difficult to find any basic similarity in the foundations for the excessive optimism of the lenders or investors. That overoptimism was necessary if the suppliers of funds were to initiate and sustain (or just participate in) the process of overlending seems evident. But the enthusiasm in each case was based on different circumstances, which varied according to episode. Take the following three instances. In the case of Asia one can argue that overoptimism was built on the observation of a success story that had lasted more than fifteen years, with average growth rates of 6–8 percent. But what can one say about Russia? When foreign investors bought massive quantities of Russian Treasury bills or equuities in 1997 they could rely only on expectations or wishful thinking—surely not on past success. As for Mexico Mark II, optimism was fuelled by the hope that liberalisation, deregulation, and privatisation would lead to future growth. In this case it is at least arguable that all these structural reforms were genuine—which, on the whole, was not the case in Russia. But even for Mexico there was little past success to rely on.

The third observation is that it is exceedingly difficult to detect a common pattern in the way debt accumulation became "unsustainable," either in fact or in the view of market participants—or both. Domestic macro policy failures, external forces beyond the control of national authorities (interest rate or terms-of-trade changes, exchange-rate gyrations, recessions), gradually emerging evidence of structural weaknesses in domestic financial intermediation, the appearance of excess capacities in key industries, the adverse effects of exchange-rate pegging, or purely political shocks—all played a role, but in shifting combinations and often reinforcing one another.

Current Account Deficits and Exchange-Rate Regimes

Large and persistent current account deficits were the rule rather than the exception. They were present before the 1982–83 Latin American, the 1994–95 Mexican and the 1997 Thai crises. They were not as significant in the case of other Asian countries, and Russia had current account surpluses; but in all these instances market participants expected (not unreasonably) either that a current account deficit would occur (Russia) or that the existing smaller ones would be aggravated (Asia). Note, however, that the chain of causality leading up to current account deficits varied substantially from case to case: there is no similarity between the twin deficit process so evident in Latin America in the late 1970s and early 1980s and Thailand's current account deficit, which accompanied domestic fiscal balance, or, indeed, Mexico's current account deficit, whose domestic counterpart was to be found predominantly in the decline of the country's saving ratio.

But in all instances, the crisis-stricken countries were operating under pegged exchange-rate regimes, with extensive—but circumvented—foreign-exchange controls in 1982–83, without them in the three other episodes. But pegging meant that when the currencies came under upward pressure during periods of strong capital inflows, the monetary authorities met with major difficulties in countering inflationary impulses without encouraging further capital inflows. And when the pressure turned downwards with the outbreak of the crisis, the result was severe—in most cases fatal—exchange-reserve losses combined with domestic interest-rate hikes that aggravated recessions.

The Role of Domestic Banking Systems

With the exception of the 1982–83 crisis, the disastrous working of domestic banking systems played a major role both in the build up of the crises and in aggravating their impact on the real economy. In Mexico and the Asian countries, reckless lending led to excessive gearing by corporations, a process which dramatically increased their fragility in the event of interest-rate increases and recession. Spectacular maturity transformation, combined with unhedged foreign-exchange positions, enhanced the vulnerability of banks themselves in the event of currency depreciation. As a result, governments found themselves in a no-win situation when the exchange rate came under pressure: neither the defence of the exchange rate through monetary tightening nor devaluation could stop the deterioration in the financial position of the banks and, either directly or indirectly (through a credit crunch), that of their customers.

The situation of the Russian banks was different, but just as bad. These banks did not play a significant role in financing the corporate sector, but their credit exposure was large enough (in relation to their own funds) and of sufficiently poor quality to make their solvency doubtful well before August 1998. Insolvency became evident once the government decided to let the rouble decline and declared a unilateral moratorium on its rouble-dominated debt-service obligations. The Russian banks carried large unhedged foreign-exchange positions and a huge Treasury bill portfolio. The large-scale bankruptcy of banks did not lead to a credit crunch; but by paralysing the domestic payment system, it had the same impact (or worse) on the real economy. In all these instances banks were operating in a substantially deregulated (or at least liberal) but poorly supervised environment.

The Outbreak of the Crisis

Dating the outbreak of a crisis is not an easy matter. A crisis can be defined as a situation where it becomes publicly known that the central bank of the country concerned has run out (or is about to run out) of reserves and could shortly become unable to service the country's foreign-currency debt obligations. When this information hits the headlines, the inflow of capital is violently reversed, domestic equity and bond markets collapse, and (barring immediate foreign assistance) the country's exchange rate plunges. On this definition, the crises reviewed in the four episodes were all sudden, brutal, and unexpected in both their timing and their violence.

But this scenario does not tell the whole story. In particular, the expression "unexpected" has to be qualified. I do not refer to the more or less veiled expressions of concern by international institutions, such as those voiced by the BIS before the 1982–83 crisis, to the confidential but reportedly strong warnings by the IMF to Thailand, or to the Fund's public critique of Russia. Yet although it is indisputable that central banks and IMF officials *did* grumble, it seems to me also fair to say that the brutality of the crises and the speed with which they spread (see below) came as a surprise to everyone, myself included.

My point about the qualified use of the word "unexpected" rather concerns the different behaviours or reaction time of market participants. The major distinction lies between domestic and foreign market participants. As already acknowledged, figures concerning capital flight by domestic market participants are notoriously difficult to obtain. Nevertheless, I venture to say that either the net outflow of private domestic capital had been a fairly steady feature for the greater part of the period of debt build up, or during the months preceding the outbreak of the crisis (as defined above), domestic private capital had started flowing out well before the reversal in net external capital flows. The first of these alternatives applied predominantly to Latin America and to Russia. The second applied to Mexico and Thailand: it would be difficult to explain the Tesobonos episode or the almost complete depletion of Thailand's net foreign-exchange reserves without such a sequence. In other words, domestic market participants held very different expectations from those of foreign lenders, or they revised their expectations earlier. However, the behaviour of foreign investors in domestic equity markets, at least in the case of Asia, came close to that of domestic market participants. As shown by the BIS Annual Report of 1998 (pp. 92–93), pension fund managers in the United States, the United Kingdom and the Netherlands began reducing their exposure to Asia as early as the last quarter of 1996, that is, at a time when banks were still busy expanding their lending to Asian borrowers. The observation that all crises tend to break out suddenly needs to be amended on at least two counts therefore.

Contagion

In all four episodes, the initial crisis tended to spread to other countries. But the direction and the intensity of contagion was by no means uniform. The contrast is particularly sharp between developments since the summer of 1998 and those before.

Mexico Mark I in 1982 carried with it practically the whole of Latin America plus a number of other developing countries, as a result of which by the spring of 1983 about two-thirds of the banking debt of the whole of the group of non-OPEC developing countries had to be rescheduled. Mexico Mark II produced its own contagion—the "tequila effect"—but this was less violent, more differentiated, and shorter-lived than the previous case. This contagion was characterised by a temporary drying-up of net capital inflows, predominantly into Latin American countries, and led to only moderate exchange-rate depreciations, the prime case being that of Brazil. On the other hand, the crisis which erupted in Thailand spread violently to Indonesia and Korea, more moderately to Malaysia and the Philippines; it affected even Hong Kong. The contagion brought with it sharp currency depreciation (except in Hong Kong), the collapse of equity prices, and a deep recession. Until the summer of 1998 this contagion did not, however, go beyond Asia. Considering the three experiences at that time, that is, before the outbreak of the Russian crisis, I was tempted to draw the rather simplistic but perhaps not completely wrong conclusion that contagion was to a large extent geographical. My thinking even applied to the first postwar sovereign debt crisis, in Poland, which also produced a regionalisation syndrome.

Contagion has manifested itself, however, in very different ways in the wake of the August 1998 Russian crisis. On the one hand, it began to threaten Latin America, most of all Brazil—despite the fact that the differences between Brazil and Russia are certainly greater than the similarities. By no stretch of imagination can this be called a "regional syndrome." At the same time, the bond, credit, and (to some extent) equity markets of the developed world started displaying characteristics which were in stark contrast to their earlier behaviour. Especially in the United States the gap between Treasury bill or bond yields and corporate bond yields widened dramatically. This flight into quality was then followed by a drastic increase in liquidity preference, so strong that the spectre of a credit crunch (which had already occurred in Japan) appeared. In short, the Russian crisis seems to have contaminated Western markets. This was a new experience: while both in 1982 and in 1994–95 there had been fears that the crisis could have systemic consequences by affecting banks or other financial institutions in the developed world, these apprehensions were defused rather quickly. There were no market developments similar in size or nature to those observed in August–October 1998. I shall say more about this in the next two chapters.

Crisis Management

One piece of information stands out in even a casual look at crisis management experiences: the staggering growth, over time, of the IMF-led rescue packages. In 1982–83 the packages granted to Mexico, Brazil, and Argentina totalled $18 billion. In 1997–98 the figure reached $118 billion for Thailand, Indonesia, and Korea. This represents a more than sixfold increase in fifteen years.

Impact on the Economies of Crisis-Stricken Countries

All four crises had a severe impact on the domestic economies of the countries involved. The Latin American crisis was followed by the "lost decade" of the 1980s, with the result that in 1990 real per capita income had just about returned to the precrisis peak. In 1995 Mexico experienced a sharp but relatively short recession. Gross domestic product in the main Asian countries hit by the crisis declined in 1998 between 5 percent and 12 percent. The Russian economy, after seven years of GDP decline, stabilised in 1997, but by the end of 1998 GDP had plunged by close to 8 percent. However, in both East Asia and Russia recovery set in early 1999.

The main conclusion of this chapter is that the large-scale accumulation of short-term external debt, which eventually became unsustainable, was at the heart of the four crises. The process leading to the build up of these debt levels varied from case to case. What mattered most was the end result: the size and the maturity profile of the external debt.

It seems possible to draw some additional conclusions, which I shall apply in the "normative" chapters, 4 and 5, to make recommendations for crisis prevention and crisis management policies. We shall have to pay particular attention (a) to the interaction between the demand for and supply of loanable funds and, within this framework, to the behaviour of international lenders and investors; (b) to the exchange-rate regime adopted by emerging market countries, and the management of their current account positions; (c) to the functioning of domestic financial intermediation in general and of the banking sector in particular, in these countries; and finally, (d) to contagion. We shall see how these preliminary conclusions will have to be altered, or extended, by looking more explicitly to the current process of financial globalisation.

3

Does Financial Globalisation Aggravate or Alleviate Market Problems?

I have presented in the previous chapter a summary of what I believe to have been the common characteristics of the four recent crises in emerging markets. In this chapter I shall move from past experience towards a discussion of the normative issues of crisis prevention and crisis handling by looking more explicitly at the implications of financial globalisation for these issues. What has been the aggravating influence of globalisation on these crises? Could it perhaps also have had an alleviating influence? And looking ahead: What could its further contribution be to the eruption of crises and their spread?

Components and Corollaries of Financial Globalisation Today

"Globalisation" is one of those inventive catchphrases of American English which convey a lot to the reader without pretending to be precise. For the purposes of this book I shall use the term in a broad sense. First I take it to mean financial integration in the geographical sense: making countries part of the global financial "village." This means that capital is free to flow between countries belonging to the globalised world, and that it does indeed flow. Controls on capital account transactions have on the whole been lifted; and current account transactions are naturally free.

But globalisation also means that these same countries have substantially liberalised, or deregulated, their domestic financial systems. This does not imply that any financial intermediary will buy or sell any financial product of its liking, but it does mean that there are few administrative restrictions in this respect. Deregulation also means that the authorities do not interfere in pricing decisions or set quantitative limits on specific lending, investing, or funding decisions. Specialisation still exists, more by tradition or free choice than as a result of regulation. But at the margin at least there is intense competition among institutions belonging to different groups of intermediaries.

The general trend towards lifting controls on capital account transactions (internationally) and deregulating financial markets (domestically) has coincided with revolutionary changes in communications and information systems technology. These changes are integral to financial globalisation today. It is to a large extent because of these changes, which have allowed the creation of highly complex new financial products and operating techniques as well as the instantaneous transmission of information, that our current global financial world is so different from the free banking and financial markets prevailing before World War I.

Let me try to list the main corollaries of globalisation. This enumeration implies no order of importance, and we must also keep in mind that many of these corollaries overlap.

1. The geographical area covered by globalisation has been growing. Globalisation started in the 1970s within what we then used to call the "industrial world," broadly speaking, the OECD area. In the second half of the 1980s it began to spread to Latin America and East Asia, and in the 1990s to Central Europe and (in a somewhat anarchical manner) to Russia.

2. There has been a substantial increase in the external exposure of financial institutions. Banks pioneered this movement in the 1970s, with a gradual increase of their external exposure both with regard to assets and in the way they managed their funding operations. External exposure may have meant cross-border or foreign-currency operations. Banks were followed by institutional investors—insurance companies, pension funds, mutual funds and, quite spectacularly, hedge funds—from the late 1980s onwards.

3. The increase in financial intermediaries' external exposure mirrored that of individual countries. One interesting (albeit partial) measure of how the "openness" of countries in terms of financial flows has changed since 1980 is the comparison over time of cross-border transactions in bonds and equities, that is, of gross purchases and sales of securities between residents and nonresidents, as a percentage of GDP. From 1980 to 1997 this ratio exploded from 9 percent to 213 percent for the United States, from 8 percent to 96 percent for Japan, from 7 percent to 253 percent for Germany, and from 5 percent to 313 percent for France.[1]

4. As a result of the combined impact of deregulation and financial innovation, there has been a gradual blurring in the neat

Table 3.1   Markets for Financial Derivative Instruments
(Notional amounts outstanding at end of year, in billions of U.S. dollars)

	1986	1988	1990	1992	1994	1996	1997
Exchange-traded instruments	583	1,300	2,284	4,634	8,863	9,870	12,207
Instruments traded over the counter	500	1,330	3,451	5,346	11,303	25,453	28,733

Source: BIS Annual reports.

distinction between various types of financial intermediaries (in particular between banks and nonbanks) as well as between various financial products.

5. Securitisation progressed throughout the 1990s, so much so that at the end of the decade the U.S. financial system had become virtually "market-centric," as opposed to the "banking-centric" system still dominating European (especially continental) financial intermediation. The exponential growth of markets for derivative instruments played a key role in this process (table 3.1). For the banks, securitisation meant that securities holdings acquired a

Table 3.2   Flow of Net International Financing
(yearly average, in billions of U.S. dollars)

	1992–93	1994–95	1996–97
Net international bank lending	182.5	260.0	460.0
Net bond and note financing	166.6	252.1	539.1

Source: BIS Annual reports.

Table 3.3   Estimated Outstanding Net Cross-Border Claims
(at end of year, in billions of U.S. dollars)

	1984	1987	1992	1997
Bank claims	1,265	2,220	3,660	5,285
Outstanding bond and note financing	410	984	1,687	3,358

Source: BIS Annual reports.

growing importance in their assets, that bank assets became more marketable, that banks were able to move from the balance sheet to off-balance-sheet commitments (or vice versa) and, more generally, that the lender-borrower relationship lost both its transparency and its stability. Internationally, the trend towards securitisation is also noticeable, though less spectacular. The flow of net bond and note financing caught up with net international bank lending by the mid-1990s, and then overtook it (table 3.2). But at end-1997 the outstanding cross-border bank claims were still significantly larger than those of outstanding bond and note financing (table 3.3).

6. Trading activities have increased tremendously, and with them the volume and average size of financial transactions. This has resulted in a spectacular surge in the volume of payments, both domestic and international. To cite just a few figures, from 1975 to 1995 the ratio of the annual volume of funds transfers (domestic and international combined) to GDP rose from 23 percent to 75 percent in the United States, from 20 percent to 105 percent in Japan, and from 10 percent to 53 percent in Germany.

7. Since the mid-1980s there has been an accelerated growth—

in absolute figures, in relation to GDP, or as a percentage of market capitalisation—of institutional investors: investment companies (basically, mutual funds), insurance companies, and pension funds. By 1995 the total assets managed by institutional investors in the United States, Canada, Japan, and Europe were estimated to have reached the equivalent of about $21 thousand billion, which substantially exceeded the total GDP of the countries concerned.[2] Half of the institutions were located in the United States, 2 percent in Canada, 14 percent in Japan, and the rest in Europe. The three kinds of institutions each accounted for around a third of the total. I have not found more recent global figures, but we know that the recent growth of their assets must have been substantial, if only because of the subsequent rise in equity prices.

To sum up in a couple of sentences the most striking outcome of these developments, one could say (a) that they have resulted in an enhanced threefold financial interdependence—geographical (between countries of the globalised world), market (for instance, between debt and equity markets), and between segments of the financial industry—and (b) that by the same token they have led to the creation of a highly competitive environment across borders, between individual financial intermediaries, and between groups of intermediaries.

With these observations in mind, let us now assess the impact of financial globalisation on crisis developments in emerging markets.

How Globalisation Makes Crisis Prevention or Handling More Difficult

Disproportion in Numbers

Probably the most important, and surely the most obvious, channel through which globalisation has made life more difficult, and is likely to make it even more so in the future, is the disproportion between the actual or potential size of capital inflows into emerging markets and that of the markets themselves. This is a sad observation, since the obvious precondition for balanced world growth is that capital flow from high-income developed countries to developing ones. And the fact that it did—especially since the early 1990s—was greeted with universal relief. Yet it would be foolish to ignore the existence of a real problem with numbers.

Although net inflows of capital into the developing world amounted to $100 billion in 1990 and $175 billion in 1993, they reached an average of about $240 billion per year during 1996 and 1997. These are, indeed, large figures, but they could become even larger in the future. A shift of 1 percent in the total assets of "Western" institutional investors towards securities purchases in emerging markets would amount to more than $200 billion; an equal shift in the gross external assets of the banks reporting to the BIS (estimated at end-1997 at $9,035 billion) would amount to another $90 billion; and a 1 percent shift in these banks' total assets would represent a multiple of this figure. I do not suggest that anything of this kind is likely to happen; but these figures show that even small changes in portfolio compositions, especially when they affect just a few emerging market countries, could severely disrupt the financial markets and the macroeconomic balance of

73

the countries concerned. The disproportion between the size of the GDP and of the domestic financial and banking market of individual (even large) developing countries on the one hand, and the lending and investing capacity of the developed countries' financial industry on the other, is staggering. This gives rise to two sets of problems.

The first is the one I have just alluded to: the capacity to absorb in an orderly way a sudden inflow of capital produced by a drastic revision of the views held by foreign lenders and investors about the prospects of the capital-importing country. Foreign direct investment would be unlikely to create many difficulties in this respect. Such investment is rarely explosive in size, and it does not require—certainly not in its "greenfield" variety—well-functioning domestic financial intermediation or capital markets. Portfolio investments and short-term bank lending are much more difficult to handle. These create problems for domestic monetary management and handling them requires sophisticated sterilisation techniques, which are not always successful and which, in turn, presuppose liquid money markets and operational expertise. More important, the absence of a developed capital market creates an incentive to convert short-term foreign exchange borrowing into long-term domestic investment. Finally, of course, both kinds of capital flows are easily reversed when unfavourable news is reported. Disproportion in numbers creates as much disruption when capital flows out as it does when capital flows in.

Although in the wake of the Mexican, Asian, and Russian crises much of this has become conventional wisdom, the impact of the disproportion in numbers may well take on other forms. This impact could be a result of a movement towards concentration within the financial industry of the developed world. If individual financial institutions in the developed world also outgrow capital-importing countries in size—and the recent wave of mergers points in that direction—the perception of risk by these institutions may be blunted. They may be ready to invest a small part of their total assets in countries heading for trouble, while at the same time these "small" investments may amount to large liabilities on the other side. As long as such investments are made in a genuinely long-term perspective, with the aim of "holding," they may have a beneficial impact on the capital-importing country's stability. But if the institutions' behaviour towards risk is asymmetrical, the result will be destabilising: the institutions will continue to lend despite warning signals and then suddenly stop and withdraw once the crisis has erupted. Thus they contribute both to the emergence of a debt bubble and to its bursting.

Global Competition: Herd Behaviour and the Search for Profit Opportunities

The reader could at this point object that the mere imbalance in numbers will contribute to the build up of unsustainable overindebtedness only if lenders or investors are specifically motivated to start directing funds towards one or more developing countries. This is a valid point—and it is at this juncture that we should consider another facet of financial globalisation. As was said above, financial globalisation has produced an exceptionally tough competitive environment. As with all competitive processes, this creates steady pressure on profit margins in well-established, traditional activities. This has led, for a number of years, to a trend of decline of the share derived from interest rate margins within banks' total profit. Ordinary wholesale banking with creditworthy national and foreign corporate customers has become, on the whole, unprofitable; and there has also been a steady squeeze on margins derived from lending to high-quality sovereign borrowers. Hence banks' efforts to raise their commission income that derived, broadly speaking, from securities transactions; hence also their often frantic search for higher returns on riskier international lending. Investment funds are equally engulfed in global competition, with similar consequences in their increased appetite for high-risk, high-yield bonds and uncertain, but potentially large, capital gains on equity or even bond investment.

It is also arguable that herd behaviour is strengthened by global competition. The greater the number of competitors—specifically, prestigious competitors—the stronger the incentive to consider that what is done by the majority will be the benchmark against which managerial performance can be evaluated. Making a mistake collectively will be judged less severely than making a mistake alone. It would take a strong conviction that everyone was wrong but oneself to act independently. Moreover, management might act on the assumption that in order to avoid systemic contagion, authorities are more likely to bail out imprudent lenders or investors when there are a lot of them. Finally, the fact that a number of prestigious institutions play an active role in the overlending process may make the others believe that these institutions know what they are doing. Whether this can be described as "rational" behaviour (as most economists now argue) depends on the meaning one gives to the word "rational." If "rational" simply means that when behaving in the way they do market participants believe that they are acting in their own interest, there may indeed be rationality in herd behaviour. But if their belief is based on false premises, their action may well produce an end result contrary to their interest—or indeed to that of a wider community. I am not sure that using the word "rational" in such circumstances adds much to our understanding of market behaviour.

Communications Technology and the Impact of the Media

Progress in communications technology—a major component of financial globalisation—has played a part in the eruption of financial crises, although I would be inclined to treat this proposition with caution. The key impact of modern communications technology is that all news becomes instantly available throughout the world. When the entire financial community learns at the same time that the central bank of a country is about to run out of foreign-exchange reserves, or when rumours of the imminent unpegging of a currency are spread worldwide, market reactions will be instantaneous and mutually reinforcing. The violence of the bursting of a debt or asset price bubble most likely increases with the speed and generalisation of information. This may be reinforced by the fact that the same technology makes it possible for large financial institutions, with establishments in widely distributed locations throughout the world, to carry out highly centralised portfolio management policies.

But the speed with which news spreads worldwide can hardly be held responsible per se for the development of excessive debt accumulation or asset price bubbles. Only rarely is all major raw news "good" and thus likely to push the majority of market participants unequivocally to act in a single direction. As we have seen in the case of Mexico Mark II, information *was* available on the growth of Mexico's current account deficit and even on the size of Tesobonos borrowings well before the eruption of the crisis; yet apparently most investors' attention was focused on "good" news rather than on this "bad" news. Similarly, all lenders or investors could read on their screen instantaneous information on BIS banking statistics during the build-up phase of Asia's debt bubble, but apparently this reading had no effect.

The point I am trying to make is that except in extreme situations—unexpectedly "good" election results or, on the contrary, the outbreak of a war or revolution—the interpretation or the selection of news matters as much as, and often more than, the news itself. Market participants are guided in these interpretations by their own past experience (or lack of it) as well as by preconceived ideas whose origins are not easy to identify. Modern communications technology and the large number of meetings, conferences, and conventions provide a good framework for harmonising such views through osmosis, which may play a significant role in strengthening herdlike behaviour. Traders and dealers are a remarkably talkative lot, and so, in a more dignified way, are analysts, bank economists, investment bankers, and even CEOs of major banks.

All of these people are also influenced, perhaps even more than by one another, by prevailing intellectual fashions. Here the main culprits are by definition economists, whose influence on market participants and officials has been vastly increased by communications technology and contemporary media. It would be worth comparing the time it took for Keynes's ideas to permeate public thinking with the much swifter impact of intellectual innovations propagated since the 1970s. The aggravating factor is provided by the unavoidable simplification required in modern communication. The pioneering work published in learned journals or books is usually highly nuanced, and the practical relevance of the propositions can be assessed by evaluating the validity of the assumptions, which are carefully laid out. Almost all this complexity disappears in television interviews or in the summaries of press agencies that appear on your computer screen. Witness the speedy acceptance of the proposition—which played a significant role in preparing for Mexico Mark II—that a current account deficit, whatever its size, does not matter as long as its domestic counterpart can be found in the saving-investment imbalance of the private sector rather than in a public-sector deficit.

Off-Balance-Sheet Activity and Securitisation Leads to the Opaqueness of Markets

The spectacular development of off-balance-sheet activities, combined with securitisation, increases the opaqueness of the marketplace. And what is even more worrying, it increases this opaqueness in such a way that there is no simple remedy. Improving disclosure and information can help, but not much.

The problem arises in the first place because the two developments combine to make the financial statements of banks (or, for that matter, of any other intermediaries) less readable. Reading a bank's balance sheet has always been a difficult exercise because so much depends on the valuation of assets, and no one can foresee the future of a credit risk. Valuation at market price helps in the sense that the reader of a balance sheet need not rely on the (possibly biased or unreliable) judgement of the bank's management. But market prices do not exist in all instances; moreover, a current market price does not reveal much about the future (what it reveals is the future as viewed by the market). This is something that should be clear by now to all the banks that took sizeable losses as a result of the collapse of, say, real estate prices. But the proliferation of off-balance-sheet, below the line, items compounds these traditional problems. Whereas the broad principles of how to value risks related to derivatives contracts are well known, there is no precise, single, standardised method of valuation, even for simple contracts. In addition, over-the-counter (OTC) contracts have long since ceased to be simple, and one would have to read the fine print before forming a view on the risk carried by the bank. No two OTC contracts are exactly the same. Heterogeneity prevails—at a time when the contribution of such contracts to banks' profits is on a sharply rising trend. To the extent that a bank discloses in detail its own methods of risk valuation, the reader of the annual reports gains some insight, but I wish him (or her) good luck when trying to assess the global creditworthiness of the reporting institution.

Off-balance-sheet activities and securitisation also lead to increasing opaqueness because for lenders and investors alike the direct credit exposure risk becomes a rapidly shrinking part of their total risk exposure. Taking the place of direct credit exposure is the indirect exposure to risk that results from the multiplicity of parties intervening in derivatives contracts.

Perhaps even more important, opaqueness affects not only the published accounts of individual institutions but also linkages between markets. Gone are the days, which were still with us at the time of the Latin American crisis in the early 1980s, when it was possible to get an idea of the exposure of a country's banking system to banks or nonbank borrowers in another country. These figures still exist—their coverage has even been improved—but they relate to on-balance-sheet items and as such cover a shrinking portion of banks' total exposure. The problem is that given the complexity of derivatives operations (some of which may involve dozens of participants), it is well-nigh impossible to work out globally significant figures relating to linkages between markets through derivatives contracts, even if it were somehow possible to collect the basic information on the micro level.

The spreading use of securities in cross-border financial transactions, even when they are unconnected with derivatives, further blurs the picture. The emerging market issuers of securities can of course be identified but not the holders. Whatever the role of institutional investors, as firm takers, underwriters, or holders of securities in proprietary trading, a high proportion of these securities end up either in offshore funds not subject to full disclosure or in household portfolios, managed or not by banks or other intermediaries.

Whereas balance-sheet opaqueness poses problems for the risk-assessment procedures of lenders and investors, unidentifiable linkages between borrowers and lenders create major headaches for crisis management. Bailing in frightened lenders is an essential ingredient of successful crisis management; and it is much easier to achieve this when the number of lenders is relatively small, well known, or ready and capable of organising themselves into a group which then becomes an efficient negotiating partner of the borrowing country or the IMF.

Let me now come to a final manifestation of opaqueness. This has to do with the fact that derivatives contracts are the main channel through which interlinkages between various markets develop, for instance, between bond and equity markets or between various segments of bond markets. New types of contracts or a sudden, unpredictable interest in a type of contract may have a major impact on asset price behaviour. It may upset patterns of asset price developments—covariances—which have hitherto been relatively stable. It may sharply increase the volatility of certain asset prices. If this happens, hedging devices based on the observation of past asset price behaviour may cease to deliver protection. In extreme cases, market liquidity may vanish.

Dangers of Contagion

There can be no doubt that financial globalisation enhances the risk of contagion. It does so almost by definition since one of the most substantive meanings of globalisation is the threefold interdependence between countries, markets, and financial industries. The contagion-breeding ability of globalisation has also been demonstrated in all four crisis episodes, even though in 1982–83 globalisation was only in its infancy.

Consider, first, the regionalisation syndrome which was conspicuous in these crises. Regional contagion may have two "rational" underpinnings. One is the assumption by foreign lenders or investors—which may or may not be true—that neighbouring countries are in a crucial sense similar to one another: the factors which drove the first country into crisis are likely to be operating in the neighbouring countries as well. The other assumption— which, again, may or may not be true—is that neighbouring countries are strongly interconnected through trade and financial flows and therefore a crisis in one of them will hit growth prospects and financial stability in the others as well. It is possible that both underpinnings are there. It is also possible that neither is present but that market participants simply believe that other market participants will act on the assumption that they are present.

Globalisation is likely to strengthen regional contagion in several ways. To the extent that it enhances trade and financial flows between neighbouring countries it will give factual support to the second assumption. It will also activate contagion by encouraging herd behaviour: if a dominant view emerges (or is thought likely to emerge) regarding the identity of the next victim, market participants will find it too risky to swim against what they believe to be the tide. Finally, investment in or lending to emerging markets is typically managed in relatively self-contained units whose performance will be evaluated by management globally. We have seen in recent years the proliferation of "emerging market indices." This kind of organisational structure promotes contagion, first regionally, and subsequently in all emerging markets.

But looking ahead, the challenging question that has arisen in the wake of the Russian crisis is whether the regional syndrome type of contagion could be overtaken by genuinely global contagion, even in the developed world, through a systemic impact on its financial intermediaries and markets. It will be a while before we fully understand what happened in the Western financial markets in the months of September and October 1998—events that prompted the expression of concern by policy makers and led the Federal Reserve Board to its threefold interest-rate cut. At the time of writing (early 1999), all I can offer is guesses, educated guesses, but guesses nevertheless.

Let us consider the channels through which crises in emerging markets could affect developed nations. The direct routes are obvious. Recession in emerging markets will have an impact on the traded goods sector of developed countries. The size of this impact, on growth and corporate profits, will depend on the number and size of the emerging markets hit by the crisis, as well as on the intensity of trade relations between the crisis-hit economies and developed countries. Japan, for instance, after having played its own part in aggravating East Asia's crisis, was in turn more affected by this crisis than the United States and Europe. The direct impact on developed countries' banks or investment funds is proportional to their exposure to the emerging market countries that are in crisis and to the nature of their crisis. Exposure to Russia, for instance, turned out to be substantial because of Russia's unilateral decision to suspend the servicing of its debt and because the rouble's plunge pushed most Russian banks into insolvency. Although all these direct impacts can do a lot of damage, it is arguable that they will not be powerful enough by themselves to throw the developed world into a global financial crisis and deep recession. I shall say more about this in the next section.

But the events of September and October 1998 have highlighted circumstances in which emerging market crisis developments could well affect the developed world. The jury is still out on how serious this risk is, or was, but we are now beginning to see that there *is* a risk.

Consider a situation in which the financial markets of the developed world have behind them a long boom period based partly on what has actually happened in the "real" economy and partly on sanguine expectations regarding the future. Price-earning ratios have reached levels that are justified only if corporate profits continue to grow indefinitely and if risk premiums on equity investment decline to zero. Business cycles are thought to have been abolished, and the possibility of unexpected "structural" changes or political backlashes is ignored. Inflation is expected to remain under control for the foreseeable future. This exuberance leaves its mark on the credit and bond markets as well. Long-term interest rates continue to decline. Interest-rate spreads between bonds issued by corporations of different credit ratings are squeezed; so are interest-rate spreads to be paid by emerging market sovereign borrowers. Here, too, the sense of risk becomes blunted—just as in the case of banks which actively search for lending possibilities at (almost) any price.

This is a world dominated by bubbles which will have to burst—a world not unlike the one preceding the August 1998 Russian crisis. That these bubbles remained intact for more than a year despite the bad news coming out of Asia is a demonstration of how deeply imbedded was the exuberance in the minds of market participants. But there had to be a last straw, and this turned out to be Russia, which appeared to set in motion the naturally bumpy process of a return to sanity. This involved an exceptionally high volatility of asset prices, the breakdown of prevailing patterns of asset price behaviour, a flight into the safest assets, and even, at a certain point, a sudden increase in liquidity preference. The risk of retrenchment by banks—a credit crunch—became significant, especially in the United States. At the time of writing (early 1999), we do not know whether the return of optimism since late October 1998 will make this episode just a temporary aberration. But we do know that a number of banks and other financial intermediaries have incurred substantial losses that go well beyond the direct impact of their exposure to emerging markets. And we also know that if the developments just mentioned were to repeat themselves, the willingness of Western institutional investors to finance the development needs of emerging market countries would vanish, and a credit crunch could do a lot of damage to the growth prospects of the United States and Europe. This would set the scene for a vicious interaction between emerging market crises and crisis manifestation in the Western world. Appropriate policy reactions in the United States, in Europe, and most importantly in Japan could, and probably would, stop this interaction developing into a full-blown world crisis and recession. But the task of crisis handling would take on a different order of magnitude from that of dealing with relatively localised emerging market crises. The main, yet still preliminary, lesson to draw from this experience is that imbalances prevailing inside the developed world provide a favourable environment for interacting with crisis eruptions in emerging markets.

In connection with dangers of contagion, payment systems deserve a special mention. As already pointed out, the spectacular surge in the volume of payments, both domestic and international, is one of the characteristic features of globalisation. This has resulted in the appearance of large intraday and very short-term liquidity and credit exposures. International credit and settlement arrangements could become the key channel for spreading a crisis across the globalised financial system. The risks tend to concentrate in the interbank large-value transfer systems, where banks face exposures on a very much larger scale than those monitored in their traditional account. Much has been done in this field, mainly as a result of central bank guidance, to limit the risk that the failure of a large market participant could spread its destabilising effects throughout the payment systems. Real-time gross settlement systems have been widely adopted, and netting systems have become markedly more robust. But there is still room for improvement, and the robustness of our systems has not yet been tested in a genuine crisis situation.

Globalisation Is a Process

Let me conclude this section by raising a broad concern. In a nutshell, it derives from the observation that financial globalisation is not a steady state but a process. We do not yet live in a single, integrated, highly competitive financial market that covers the whole world, a market which would be basically deregulated and free from capital controls yet where a common understanding would prevail about the rules of the game. We have been *moving* in that direction, but the target is far from reached, and arguably it will take a long time to reach it, if we ever do. As everyone should know by now, a lot of things can happen on the way to the forum. Let me spell out this concern in some detail.

By way of introduction, however, I offer a few remarks concerning the goal of a fully competitive, deregulated, integrated international financial system where capital and information flow freely. As in all economic activities, competition brings numerous benefits to the consumers, in this case, the users of financial services. It increases the range of financial products, adapts them to the needs of lenders and borrowers, and allows the markets to respond swiftly to shifts in demand and supply. It leads to a better allocation of resources worldwide and therefore enhances growth prospects. In other words, it increases economic efficiency in the narrow technical sense used by economists as well as in the broad, commonsense meaning of the term.

Describing the working of competition in this way is probably uncontroversial as far as it goes, but it does not go far enough. Competition goes hand in hand with pressure on profits: it is because of this pressure that financial firms will act inventively for the benefit of consumers and will want to make the best use of scarce resources. A good thing for the users of financial services, but not so painless for financial firms. The pressure on profit margins is not a gentle process, affecting all firms gradually and uniformly. It varies over time, accelerates violently, and affects differently various types of activities—especially in a world dominated by technological change and financial innovation. The essence of competition is Schumpeter's "creative destruction." The emergence of new products, new firms, or new branches of activity carries with it the disappearance of outdated products and the often brutal elimination of individual firms or even of segments of the industry. Without such "destruction" the economy will be unable to fully benefit from the "creative" facets of competition. Creativity is not compatible with a peaceful life.

The crucial question, then, is whether "destruction" in the world of finance implies a greater risk of systemic instability than it does for say, manufacturers of engineering products or microchips. It may well do so. Hence the conclusion, to which I shall return in the next chapters, that even if we were to reach a state of generalised competition on a worldwide scale, financial markets ought not to be left to their own devices. Those who attribute the virtues of global stability to a fully competitive and liberalised financial system may be right. But how can we know? Surely not on the basis of theoretical models, which are always founded on well-defined but usually restrictive assumptions. I do not think we know the answer. But neither do I believe that we should try to find out in practice how smoothly and swiftly self-correcting our system would be in the absence of the active care of the public authorities.

Be that as it may, the more important point I would like to make is that the question of how to operate a fully liberalised system worldwide is not the most urgent one. Such a system may or may not be unstable. But I am sure that moving towards that (uncertain) utopian state carries with it the risk of heightened instability. Our more practical concern should be to manage the transition from here to there.

In all four crises the mismanagement of liberalisation played a role—admittedly, not an easily quantifiable one—in the build up of unsustainable overindebtedness. Although in 1982–83 the Latin American countries were not in the process of liberalising their financial systems, the Western banking system, though in most cases still highly regulated in domestic activities, was beginning to enjoy great freedom in international lending. Claims on non-OPEC developing countries of the banks reporting to the BIS grew from $32 billion at end-1973 to $247 billion at end-1982, an annual rate of close to 25 percent. This was a rate which probably could not have been accompanied by an appropriate adjustment of banks' international credit risk-assessment capability. In the early 1990s, deregulation in Mexico materially contributed to the ill-managed explosion of bank credit; and in Asia, maturity and currency mismatching by banks, which had just acquired a high degree of freedom, played a major role in making the external debt accumulation unsustainable. As for Russia, institution-building and the establishment and enforcement of clear rules, for instance regarding the management of foreign-currency indebtedness, lagged dramatically behind the degree of freedom acquired by Russian financial institutions.

It is worth noting that in a number of instances, banking or financial crisis manifestation within Western countries coincided with the process of liberalisation or deregulation. This was the case in the United States with the savings and loans industry, or in the Nordic countries, notably Sweden, with the banking industry.

In all instances, the problems appear to have originated in a similar way. Deregulation opens up profit opportunities and at the same time raises competitive challenges. The abolition of quantitative credit controls is a good example of the first impact; the removal of interest-rate ceilings on deposit-taking is the simplest example of the second. Adjustment to such influences requires in all cases drastic and long-lasting institutional changes, but adjustment becomes even more difficult when deregulation is asymmetrical, for instance when sharply increased competition on the funding side is not accompanied by the opening up of new profit opportunities on the assets side of the balance sheet.

The crux of the matter is that the transition from a tightly controlled to a deregulated environment not only requires a well-thought-out, well-managed process of deregulation; it also requires simultaneously broad institutional adjustment in a number of key areas: for existing institutions the "management culture" has to change, in particular in risk-assessment and risk-control procedures; an appropriate institutional framework has to be set up that allows for the creation of new institutions, for instance, mutual funds or other institutional investors needed for a well-functioning capital market; the legal framework has to be revised, in particular, in the field of bankruptcy procedures; and the regulatory system has to be adapted and the new regulations enforced. Institution building on this scale takes time, and developing a new managerial class takes even more. Only if that time is taken can one hope to tip the cost-benefit balance of deregulation towards a net gain in benefits. But the wisdom to recognize this is a rare commodity. The danger is particularly acute when a number of macroeconomic indicators paint a rosy picture, as was the case for Mexico and even more so for the Asian countries. For it is precisely in a favourable macroeconomic situation, with rising financial and real asset prices, when the perception of risk is blunted, that the temptation arises to let liberalisation run ahead of institution-strengthening groundwork.

The process of transition towards worldwide financial integration carries another, less technical but possibly even greater, challenge, in particular for investors or lenders in developed market economies. This challenge is caused by the spread of globalisation. As more and more countries join the global village, those in charge of lending or investing decisions in the new emerging markets cannot simply rely on facts and figures, even if these figures are reliable. Investors certainly, but also lenders, need a genuine understanding of how different countries function in reality. Differences between two emerging markets located in the same geographical area can be enormous—as all those in charge of sorting out the mess in Asia now realise. But the human resources needed to supply this in-depth knowledge are not there; and acquiring these resources will again take time. Where are the people who would be capable of assessing the risks of China or India joining the world of financial globalisation?

The Alleviating Impact of Globalisation

Some of the advocates of financial globalisation would argue that in addition to the efficiency-raising benefits it has brought to the world economy—which are taken for granted by most economists and policy makers (myself included)—globalisation will also tend to enhance stability. It will do so because in a liberalised and deregulated, and therefore highly competitive, environment the self-correcting forces of the market will be allowed to do their job. I explained above why I have doubts about the practical relevance of this very general assertion: first, I am not sure that even a fully globalised financial system will behave in this way and, second, I am quite sure that the road to that supposedly desirable state will be bumpy. Be that as it may, I nonetheless do share the view that globalisation, even at this stage of its development, contains components which act in a stabilising way. Most of these are the opposite aspect of the destabilising factors enumerated in the previous section. The difficulty is to find out which of the two opposing influences is likely to prevail.

The Potentially Alleviating Impact of Size Disparity

One such influence can be found in the size disparities mentioned earlier. The very large size of Western banks or other financial intermediaries in comparison with their loans to, or investments in, individual emerging markets may steer these institutions towards reckless risk taking. But conversely, should there be adverse developments, this same size differential may induce the banks to hold on to their assets or to roll over, say, their interbank loans when invited to participate in IMF-organised rescue packages. These banks do not have to cut their losses; they can afford to take a long view. By the same token, even generous provisioning will not put their own creditworthiness at risk. They will not become part of a chain reaction leading to global contagion. The contrast between the current Asian crisis and the Latin American crisis in the early 1980s is telling: at that time the claims of the main U.S. banks on crisis-hit Latin American countries were well in excess of the banks' equity, while today the exposure of the largest U.S. banks to the five Asian countries is much smaller; even a generalised crisis in Latin America today would not expose them to the risk they carried in 1982. The very fast growth of the developed countries' financial "superstructures" combined with bank mergers and the substantial increase in banks' capital ratios has radically changed the relative orders of magnitude since that time.

In my more optimistic moments I would also like to believe that the spreading internationalisation of banks and other institutions, such as investment banks, has educated them. One might hope that institutions which for some years have been effectively operating in a number of countries might have learnt to differentiate among these countries and will therefore be less inclined to succumb to manifestations of regional syndromes. But on this point my optimism is limited. Not that I question the ability of individual institutions to learn, but that globalisation implies the growing participation of inexperienced financial businesses whose unwarranted behaviour may incite even the more experienced businesses to go along with them. Herd behaviour may be contagious in all directions.

Wider Distribution of Risks

The number and composition of lenders and investors are likely to have an additional alleviating impact by putting a further brake on contagion. This has to do not so much with the fast growth in the size of individual lenders or investors as with the increased participation of nonbank financial intermediaries—notably institutional investors—in international lending. This participation distributes the financial impact of losses initiated by a financial crisis in an emerging market more evenly. Consider, again, the contrast between 1982–83 and the current Asian crisis. That the latter had a more benign impact on banks should be attributed not only to the much larger size of the individual banks but also to the fact that a high proportion of the actual or potential losses are now being borne by holders of bonds and equity. This spreading-out process has been reinforced by securitisation, which allowed banks to sell to investors part of their claims on emerging market debtors.

Role of Equity Purchases by Western Investors

When the diversification of capital flows to emerging market countries constitutes a rising proportion of equity inflows, this too can have a smoothing influence on the contagion effect of a crisis. Some such influence may be detected in the Asian case. The inflow of bank and bond finance into the five Asian countries during the seven-year period 1990–96 amounted to $240 billion. During the same period, the net equity inflow was estimated at $89 billion—quite a large sum.[3] As already mentioned, the net equity inflow dried up much earlier than bank and bond finance, which is perhaps a tribute to the forecasting ability of equity portfolio managers, but which by the same token put much of the responsibility for the impending stock market crash on the shoulders of foreign investors. But the other side of the coin is that while foreign equity holders also incurred substantial losses,[4] those losses had no noticeable impact on Western equity markets or, more broadly, on financial stability, as they would have done had the losses been incurred by, say, banks.

Financial Innovations as Hedging Devices

Finally, there is a ray of hope: financial innovations can be used as hedging devices. I mentioned my concern about the opaqueness produced by the spectacular development of derivatives. But this should not hide the fact that interest rate or currency swaps or futures, or much more sophisticated derivatives contracts linked to equity markets or designed to protect banks against credit risks, can be used as powerful hedging devices which enable wise financial market participants to protect themselves against unforeseen asset price volatility.

These hedging operations can be viewed as insurance policies: they are taken out by risk-averse market participants. But they have also to be considered in a global context. The global marketplace cannot insure itself against a risk. When a banking system collapses, there will be a net loss for the global village. The decline in financial asset prices implies a decline in financial wealth. What insurance can do is shift the burden of such losses from risk-averse market participants to willing risk takers. If those risk takers know what they are doing and correctly assess their ability to withstand losses, the redistribution of risk will allow the system as a whole to gain in stability, and the impact of financial wealth losses on the "real" economy will be smaller than it would otherwise have been.

We cannot know, however, how effective this smoothing influence will be. It depends crucially on the wisdom of risk takers. Accepting the role of insurers against equity or bond price volatility in a world moving towards globalisation is not at all the same as issuing a life insurance policy. Patterns of asset price behaviour may be subject to radical changes. Covariances may break down, while new ones emerge. This can play havoc with risk-diversification and risk-hedging strategies. To put it mildly, we have more experience with mortality tables, automobile accidents, even natural disasters, than with asset price behaviour in periods of financial instability during globalisation. With the novel experience of globalisation, history will not necessarily provide guidance, yet if insurers cannot rely on past experience, what else can they look to?

With an eye on desirable and possible policy reactions to financial crises in emerging market countries I shall now try to draw some conclusions regarding the impact of financial globalisation on these crises. This builds on what I believe to have been the common factors of the four crises. Building on such foundations is a risky enterprise; the specificities of each crisis have been so varied and changeable that what in the past has been a standard feature may well vanish in the future. The whole enterprise becomes even more hazardous when one realises that some of the key features of financial globalisation which already have played—and are likely to play in the future—an aggravating role may at the same time alleviate crisis manifestations.

The first bad news is that with financial globalisation spreading to more and more emerging market countries and penetrating ever more deeply into their domestic economies, there is an increasing rather than a decreasing probability that financial crises will continue to erupt in these countries. There are two reasons for this. Both have to do with the likely, repeated "unsustainable" debt accumulation which has been a key common feature of precrisis scenarios in all four crisis episodes. First, globalisation has increased the possibility of overlending to emerging markets by financial institutions from the developed countries: see the already prevailing disproportion in numbers and the growing appetite of institutional investors for international investment. At the same time, it has also provided the incentive for this overlending: see the frantic search for profit opportunities in the wake of competitive pressure on "traditional" activities and the opinion-forming bias of a world dominated by instantaneous, global communications. The second reason is that the capacity of emerging markets to absorb capital inflows in an orderly way just does not keep pace with the potentially explosive increase of such inflows. This capacity is constrained by the countries' inability to handle the macro policy challenges raised by sudden, large capital inflows. It is also constrained by the time-consuming process of building an efficient, diversified and well-supervised domestic system of financial intermediation. An aggravating factor is that lenders and investors will find it hard to identify these constraints for specific countries and will therefore be unable to evaluate the risks implied by their own decisions for the countries concerned and, eventually, for themselves.

By making this point, I do not suggest that in a longer perspective emerging market countries would lose by entering the global financial marketplace. Over time not only capital imports as such but the broader efficiency impact of financial globalisation will lead to a higher rate of growth than if the economies remained closed in terms of the capital account of the balance of payments. But, again, the bad news is that the trend is likely to be interrupted, at best by short but violent recessions or at worst by deep recessions followed by a longer period of stagnation in real per capita income.

More bad news is that once a crisis erupts, it will spread through contagion to other emerging markets. Globalisation is likely to speed up this process of contagion. As noted above, a more intimate knowledge of individual emerging market economies might encourage some differentiation and therefore act as a brake on contagion; but there is a lot of evidence to suggest that when investors see their equity or bond investments in all emerging market countries as a group or as a class, contagion will prevail over differentiation.

The list of "bad news" items looks impressive, and it *is* impressive. Could they not be offset, to some extent at least, by the crisis-alleviating factors listed above? I have mentioned four of them: the shrinking of the emerging market exposure of Western lenders and investors relative to the size and the capital endowment of these institutions; the growing importance of market-centric (as opposed to bank-centric) finance, which leads, among other things, to a wider distribution of risk; in this category, the increasing role of equity investment; and finally, the risk-insurance opportunities provided by financial innovations. The common feature of these alleviating influences seems to be that they tend to strengthen the financial systems of the developed world against financial shocks emanating from emerging market economies. Contagion to other emerging markets may be activated by financial globalisation but perhaps the opposite holds for the developed world. One would be tempted to draw the conclusion that the risk of a full-blown, global systemic crisis has receded.

But has it? I was tempted to believe this myself until the outbreak of the Russian crisis—or, more precisely, until the appearance of "unusual strains" in the U.S. financial markets in September–October 1998, which prompted the U.S. monetary authorities to cut interest rates and to engineer (or facilitate) the Long-Term Capital Management (LTCM) rescue operation. Significantly, they even added a third rate cut in November, that is, at a time when the Dow Jones index had already been quite close to its precrisis bubble peak. The expression "unusual strain" figured in the communiqué announcing this move.

The U.S. market developments—high volatility of asset prices, significant increases in risk premiums, flight into quality and liquidity, the risk of a credit crunch or at least of a policy of retrenchment—raise two intriguing questions. I expounded one of them above: Can one argue that the impact of the Russian crisis was so strong because of the existence of several bubbles in the U.S. markets which would have burst anyhow? If this were so, the lesson would be straightforward: the best way to limit the risk of contagion is to avoid bubbles. The other question arises when one considers the fact that these unusual strains were concentrated in the U.S. market; European markets remained largely immune. Why was this so? The U.S. institutions do not appear to have been more heavily exposed to Asia than European ones; and their direct exposure to Russia was probably less. Did the market fear a large-scale contagion extending to Brazil and perhaps to the whole of Latin America? Or has this strange asymmetry something to do with the market-centric development of U.S. financial intermediation? The mere fact that I raise this second question might be regarded as iconoclastic. Why should a market-centric system be more sensitive to shocks originating in emerging markets, especially when the direct exposure to these countries is arguably quite limited?

4

Crisis Prevention

The gist of the argument developed in the preceding chapter is that financial globalisation enhances the probability that crises will continue to erupt in emerging markets—not a very original conclusion when one looks at what has been happening since the mid-1990s. But recognition of the crisis-breeding proclivities of globalisation does not imply that we must regard such crises as unavoidable. On the contrary, it should lead us to consider, and implement, crisis-prevention policies. I have two caveats, however. We should entertain no illusion about our ability to prevent all crises, and we should not think that the full elimination of crisis manifestations would necessarily be desirable. In our market economies, crises play, as they always did, a useful role in correcting policy mistakes (some of which will always occur) or adjusting the misallocation of resources produced by boom conditions (and that will also recur). Distortions are inevitable even in well-functioning market economies, and it is clearly better to eliminate them at an early stage, even if the elimination does not go smoothly, rather than let them acquire a dimension and complexity which could ultimately lead to a truly unmanageable crisis.

That being said, a more modest assignment for crisis prevention would be threefold: first, to reduce the probability that a large-scale crisis will hit one of the emerging market economies—and we have seen that the major cause of severe crisis eruptions has in the past been the appearance of debt or asset price bubbles which, for various reasons, became unsustainable in the eyes of market participants; second, to enhance the resilience of these economies to crisis manifestations; and third, to limit the chances of contagion both to other emerging markets and to the developed world. With these partly overlapping objectives in mind, what courses of action can we envisage? I shall go from what I consider the less to the more controversial recommendations.

Sound Macro Policies

Advocating sound, that is, stability-oriented monetary and fiscal policies would have been a self-evident proposition before Mexico Mark II and the East Asian crises. Current account deficits brought about by fiscal profligacy and high, often accelerating inflation produced by loose monetary policies were seen to be at the root of the process that eventually led to crisis. Hence the standard practice of the IMF to combine a financing facility with strict conditions based on two pillars: fiscal restraint and monetary tightening. Hence also the perception that the best way to avoid crises is to practise a conservative monetary policy combined with a responsible fiscal policy.

This (almost) conventional wisdom came to be questioned first after the 1994–95 Mexican crisis. Before the crisis, inflation had been decelerating in Mexico to single-digit figures and fiscal policy could be regarded as responsible. The questioning became even more vocal after the crises which hit a number of Asian countries in 1997. Before these crises, East Asian countries had on the whole pursued satisfactory macroeconomic policies, generated exceptionally high domestic saving ratios (this had not been the case in Mexico), tolerated—with the exception of Thailand—moderate current account deficits (again, not the case in Mexico), and had behind them a long period of exceptionally fast growth which made them the envy of all other emerging market countries. These observations would seem to warrant the view that the insistence on prudent macro policies as the most important crisis-prevention mechanism has outlived its justification or should at least be relegated to a second-order consideration. I regard this conclusion, even in its watered-down version, as dangerously wrong.

For one thing, I do not believe that we should take it for granted that the current consensus on the virtues of fiscal rectitude and stability-oriented monetary policy will always prevail. It is true that we have witnessed, first among the developed countries and later among a great number of emerging market economies, a welcome conversion to this kind of policy correctness. But whether this attitude will continue is an open question—and by underplaying its importance in crisis-prevention policies we would not increase its chances of survival. Moreover, if we needed a reminder that ill-conceived, or ill-implemented, fiscal policies have not disappeared as one of the major sources of financial crisis, the current Russian situation has delivered a forceful reminder. And Brazil has revived, quite rightly, the twin deficit argument.

But there is more to my reluctance to go along with the rejection of the older conventional wisdom. It would be wrong to judge the crisis-breeding capacity of a lax monetary policy solely on the basis of the observed rates of increase in the consumer price index. Both in Mexico and in most Asian countries hit by the crisis, the rate of growth of bank credit before the crisis had been exceptionally fast. Judged by this criterion, monetary policy could hardly be regarded as having been cautious. Some of this credit expansion may have been part of a onetime structural adjustment: banking reintermediation in the wake of deregulation. Be that as it may, there can be no doubt that the budget constraint on households and nonfinancial firms was considerably eased. Admittedly, this did not reflect itself in any acceleration of price inflation (as measured by the CPI), but it surely contributed to the real estate and equity market bubbles. Price inflation was kept under control by exchange-rate pegging and the resulting real appreciation.

Just as the stance of monetary policy cannot be judged by looking solely at the CPI, that of fiscal policy cannot be evaluated unequivocally by looking at the fiscal balance defined in one single way. In a period of speedy privatisation, when government-owned (but off-budget) development banks play a significant role in the flow of funds, several fiscal balance definitions are needed to assess the income- and expenditure-generating effect of fiscal policy.

Finally, the need to pursue stability-oriented macro policies does not apply solely to crisis-prone emerging markets. What matters just as much is the successful pursuit of such policies by large developed countries whose policies are liable to have a major impact on the external environment in which emerging market countries operate. We saw in Chapter 1 the devastating impact during the late 1970s and early 1980s of U.S. monetary policy on Latin America when a period of laxity was followed by a sharp tightening. We also noted the impact of the gyrations in the yen-dollar exchange rate as well as of Japan's recession (which itself owes a lot to the bursting of an earlier asset price bubble) on crisis-hit Asian countries.

These two examples reveal, however, the complexity of the problem. The first case was relatively simple, analytically at least, though clearly not politically. Monetary policy in the United States was too loose in the late 1970s. Because market participants did not yet realize that their expectations were supposed to be rational, the policy produced negative real interest rates by all definitions, and significantly contributed to the appearance of a borrowers' market in international bank lending. The United States (and the debtor countries) had to pay the price for this misunderstanding when U.S. monetary policy belatedly became restrictive; and the price was probably increased by the inappropriate U.S. policy mix, which combined monetary restraint with fiscal laxity. I do not suggest that it would have been easy to avoid this sequence of events; but at least we know (and not only with hindsight) what went wrong, and we may hope that such an experience will not be repeated.

The second example, on the other hand, raises more intricate analytical questions, which do not help solve problems related to policy feasibility. What created Japan's asset price bubble, whose bursting has still not been accommodated by the Japanese economy? Probably an overly easy monetary policy—but then why did this policy have no impact on Japanese CPI inflation? Even if we knew the answer to that, should we draw the conclusion that monetary policy ought specifically to target asset price stability?

But this is only half of the problem raised by the case of Japan. There is also the question of whether policy makers in the principal countries should attempt to stabilise exchange rates, or at least try to avoid major, disruptive real exchange-rate misalignments. That large and lasting misalignments between the major floating currencies—the dollar, the yen and the euro—can have damaging effects on the "real" economy is, to my mind, indisputable. They can disrupt emerging markets, as we have seen in the case of Asia. They can also have adverse effects on the developed countries by producing a misallocation of resources, raising uncertainty, and encouraging protectionist backlashes. And the trouble is that even modern financial engineering has not yet invented hedging devices against deep, lasting real exchange-rate misalignments; and when it does, my guess is that it will be prohibitively expensive. So there are plenty of valid arguments in favour of trying to stabilise real exchange-rate relations between the major currencies.

What is questionable, however, is our ability to do so. Exchange-market intervention may simply accelerate a turnaround in the exchange rate that would have happened anyway (just a little later). Its impact will otherwise be only temporary, except when market participants are made to believe that it signals a change in macroeconomic policies and, most important, in monetary policy. This boils down to saying that exchange-rate stabilisation requires a high degree of coordination of monetary and fiscal policies. What are the chances of coordinating, say, U.S. and European macroeconomic policies? Pretty small, unless there are converging *domestic* reasons on both sides for doing so. It is only then that exchange-market intervention would send a credible signal to market participants that intervention would be followed by jointly agreed shifts in macroeconomic policy mixes. Take, as an example, the situation prevailing at present (early 1999). To stop the slide of the euro against the dollar (or, what amounts to the same, the rise of the dollar against the euro), the European Central Bank would have to raise its interest rate while the Fed lowered its own. Clearly, this would go against the domestic interests of both areas. It is even arguable that considerations relating to domestic balance would suggest doing the opposite.

It is just conceivable—but not more—that the introduction of the euro will enhance the chances of a balanced policy coordination between the United States and Europe. The degree of openness of the euro area has now become similar to that of the United States: foreign trade amounts to around 10 percent of gross domestic product. This means that exchange-rate fluctuations could have the same sort of influence on domestic price formation. At the same time, the development of a large, liquid, and transparent market for euro-denominated government paper may provide a genuine alternative to investments in the U.S. Treasury bill and bond market. This may happen faster than expected, and could moderate the U.S. authorities' propensity towards benign neglect in the presence of a declining dollar. Both developments could eventually lead to a situation in which both the United States and the euro area would acquire a genuine interest in coordinating their policies and, moreover, would do so in a position of power balance.

Well-Functioning Domestic Financial Intermediation

It is now generally recognised that inadequate or faulty domestic financial intermediation may bear some responsibility for (a) increasing the likelihood that an emerging market economy will be hit by a major crisis; (b) weakening its capacity to manage such a crisis in a way that would moderate its impact on the "real" economy; and (c) amplifying the risk of contagion. This view was first mooted after the Mexican crisis of 1994–95; it gained considerable strength after the eruption of the Asian crisis, and became obvious to anyone who cared to look at what was happening in Russia. I share the view with one major proviso: while inadequate or faulty intermediation does indeed bear the threefold responsibility just defined, it does not follow that a crisis could not erupt in countries endowed with a reasonably well-functioning system of financial intermediation or that crisis management will be costless. Sweden went through an expensive financial crisis in 1991–93, and in the United States the cost of resolving the banking and savings and loans crises between 1980 and 1992 added up to the equivalent of 3 percent of the 1992 GDP. Admittedly, neither in Sweden nor in the United States could financial intermediation be considered at that time as faultless, but in terms of efficiency and resilience it was surely light years ahead of financial intermediation in any emerging market.

The challenge faced by emerging market countries is to define the guidelines for improving the functioning of their system of domestic financial intermediation. One part of this task is uncontroversial, even though implementation will be difficult and take years. This concerns improvements in (or in some cases the establishment of) what I would loosely call the legal and institutional preconditions, or infrastructure, for the proper working of financial markets. Some of the most important are a well-designed and enforced corporate law, accounting and disclosure standards, clear definition of property rights, a solid legal framework for commercial and financial contracts; legal dispositions regarding the constitution and disposal of collateral; bankruptcy rules and procedures; prudential rules for the various categories of financial market participants; enforced supervision of those participants; liquid and transparent organised exchanges; well-functioning payment, clearing and settlement systems; and, of course, adequate corporate governance. I do not propose to discuss these components of the legal-institutional framework, not because they lack importance (they don't) nor because their implementation is easy (it isn't) but because setting up these institutional pillars has by now been recognised as a prerequisite for any well-functioning system of financial intermediation.

Much more controversial is the definition of the broad structure of financial intermediation that one would recommend emerging markets to adopt. Should this structure favour a market-centric approach as opposed to a bank-centric one? If so, should the functioning of markets be supported by the deliberate development of institutional investors? What sort of protection (if any) should be given to households induced to invest in markets—especially in equity markets? Assuming that banks will continue to play an important (if not exclusive or dominant) role in financial intermediation, should they be restrained from underwriting and selling securities or allowed to buy and sell the full range of financial products? What sort of linkages should be allowed (or encouraged) between banks, nonbank financial firms or nonfinancial businesses? How should prudential supervision be organised, and what institution should exercise it?

I find it difficult to answer these questions with any degree of certainty for several reasons. For one thing, no established, commonly accepted model exists in the developed world. Admittedly, the trend towards deregulation has been steady and fairly general, but when it comes to the specificities of this process, there are still sizeable differences between, say, the United States and continental Europe. There is no doubt that with the much faster development of securities markets and the much wider spread of equity ownership, the United States is well ahead of Europe in moving towards a basically market-centric system. On the other hand, the participation of banks in underwriting and selling securities is far more advanced in Europe, both because of the historical tradition of universal banking and because of the way deregulation has been taking place in Europe. Equally, some types of linkages between banks and nonbanking financial firms (such as mergers—not simply operational links—between banks and insurance companies) have been more common in Europe than in the United States. But a closer look would also reveal differences between European countries, especially between the United Kingdom and continental Europe.

There is a second, perhaps more important reason for my reluctance to dictate the appropriate financial structures for emerging economies. Even if we were able to identify a model towards which emerging market countries should move, this would still not authorise us to ignore the time required to reach this objective. Consider the evident need for all these countries to establish and nurture a strong and varied SME (small and medium sized enterprise) sector. The financial structure which would seem to be the most helpful for achieving this target is one that could provide equity financing for this sector. The provision of risk capital is best ensured in the United States. But would it be realistic to expect that the U.S. experience could be copied successfully and on a large scale in countries with a much less advanced equity culture, even for the financing of large enterprises? An intermediate, second-best solution might be a traditional branch-banking network, which can combine the advantages of customer proximity with a more sophisticated supply of financing packages.

In addition, Western advisers should bear in mind that imprudent risk taking has not been, to put it mildly, the privilege of banks in emerging markets. I do not refer here to the active participation of Western banks or other financial institutions in the process of overlending to Latin America, Asia, or Russia, something that can perhaps be explained by the development of globalisation, as I tried to show previously. What I have in mind are the numerous cases of imprudent lending to domestic borrowers or corporations operating in other Western countries and, moreover, in traditional areas, such as real estate financing. I referred at the beginning of this chapter to the Swedish and the U.S. savings and loans crises. I could just as well mention the case of Crédit Lyonnais (whose rescue may well cost French taxpayers up to $20 billion) and, recently, the involvement of banks in the financing of LTCM in the United States. What is most worrying in the latter case is the evident failure to follow the most elementary rule of banking: ask the right questions before granting credit. The silver lining is the fact that because of the considerable improvement of banks' capital base during the past decade the recent manifestations of imprudence have not put the very existence of banks at risk as they did, say, in the case of Sweden. But we also have to bear in mind that the improvement of capital ratios can be attributed just as much to the action of public authorities as to the enlightened policy of bank managements.

However troublesome the implications of these observations, we cannot avoid addressing the problems that arise for emerging market countries as a result of inadequate financial intermediation. But we should do so in a pragmatic way, seeking to bring remedies to identified weaknesses, without the excessive ambition of a global solution, which in the end could turn out to be unrealisable or even mistaken. In what follows, I shall try to outline a few courses of action.

1. Banks in Mexico, Asia, and Russia contributed variously but massively to the emergence of lending, equity, and real estate bubbles by disregarding elementary rules of prudent management. In all cases they took on excessive exchange-rate risks; in many cases they undertook reckless maturity transformation; and generally, they disregarded credit risks. The experience of the Russian banks is worth remembering. The amount of credit they extended played only a marginal role in financing the corporate sector, but it was large enough for the banks themselves to be pushed towards insolvency even before they were hit by the decisions of the Russian government in August 1998. To the extent that there were other financial intermediaries (for example, finance companies in Thai-

land), these institutions mismanaged their business in the same way. So the first task is to impose on these institutions—and to enforce—tight prudential rules. We can hope that managements will have learned lessons and drawn appropriate conclusions. But countries cannot rely on this assumption. Prudential rules should be strict and unambiguous, and they should be enforced by supervisors on the basis of frequent and detailed reporting, supported by on-site inspection where necessary. This should apply not only to countries which have gone through, or are in, a crisis situation but also to those in the process of liberalisation. I would find it ludicrous to advocate that the banking systems of emerging countries adopt the kind of supervisory philosophy now being proposed for developed countries, in which the choice of risk-assessment and risk-control systems should be left to the banks themselves, leaving the supervisors to make sure that the systems are in place and effectively operating.

2. There has been widespread (though for obvious reasons mainly anecdotal) evidence of banks extending credit, or taking on other kinds of risk, under pressure from governments or because of their links to industry or commerce. The first of these influences can be eliminated only through privatisation; but the second contains a useful reminder that the way private ownership is established, or exercised, counts just as much as the fact of privatisation itself. This raises two distinct but in practice interrelated issues: banks' links with nonbanking and, in particular, nonfinancial enterprises; and corporate governance. In this field, as in that of supervision, I would caution against transplanting indiscriminately practices or trends that have recently prevailed in developed countries. Combining industry or commerce with banking created a

host of problems (not entirely dissimilar from those observed in Mexico, Asia, and Russia) in most developed countries during the 1929–33 crisis, and this resulted in many cases in a regulatory backlash. The trend has been reversed since then, probably even more radically in Europe than in the United States. There may be some justification for this change of attitude because most of the dangers arising out of links between banks and (especially) nonfinancial firms are likely to be neutralised by the improvement in disclosure obligations and practices, self-imposed "Chinese walls" discipline and, most important, improved corporate governance which, among other things, clearly defines the respective responsibilities of shareholders and management. However, even in the developed world, only time will tell if this potential neutralisation will be effective. I would consider this route dangerous at the present stage of development of the emerging markets. Better corporate governance, better disclosure, and better internal management practices should precede, not follow, the establishment of links between banks and industry. Hence, at this stage, dominant (direct or indirect) shareholding by nonfinancial firms in banks should be prohibited, and banks' holding of equity in nonbanks should equally be subject to strictly enforced quantitative regulations.

3. Such a proposition, of course, immediately raises the politically sensitive issue of foreign ownership of banks. In most emerging market countries, financial wealth which would be independent of nonfinancial activities, and sizeable enough to take control of banks simply does not exist. The development of institutional investors—pension funds, insurance companies, investment funds—will take time; so will the possibility of selling bank shares to a large number of small private shareholders. The

only way of ensuring large-scale, effective, and safe privatisation is to allow banks from developed countries to become dominant shareholders in the domestic banking systems of emerging countries. Several more positive arguments can be advanced in support of such a course of action. For example, it would amount to transferring a superior risk-management and credit culture to emerging markets, the acquisition of which would otherwise take many years. Although recent events tend to weaken the persuasiveness of this argument, the gist of it probably still remains true. Even more convincing is the argument that such a privatisation would mean the import of technological and professional know-how, thus saving emerging markets years of trouble "inventing" what has already been invented. Finally, and most important, such shareholdings would provide domestic banks with a capital base which would substantially enhance their resilience in a situation of economic and financial fragility. For good or bad reasons, so far only a few countries have agreed to follow this route without reservation: Hungary, Argentina, and more recently Mexico.

The main reason behind the politically motivated reluctance to allow foreign ownership in domestic banks is the belief that banks are the source of considerable power, which can be misused by foreigners against the national interest. How to respond to this seemingly reasonable concern? First, in all those emerging market countries where banking power was misused, the abuse was performed by nationals: the government itself or private owners. Second, the best way of limiting potential misuse of banking power is to curtail it by severing links between banks and nonfinancial firms, as I suggested above. Third, an additional protection against excessive power is the stimulation of competition. Monopoly positions should be avoided. Competition among several foreign-owned banks would go a long way towards ensuring that banks act in their customers' interest. Finally, I could see some advantages in privatisation procedures which demand that foreign owners of banks come from different countries and fill the gap in servicing the SME sector.

4. Let me now turn to a much broader, more complex, and probably more controversial set of issues. Would it help crisis prevention if equity markets were given a significantly greater role in the process of financial intermediation in emerging markets?

One would be tempted to answer this question in the affirmative since excessive leverage has borne considerable responsibility for aggravating the crisis in all four historical episodes. What emerging markets really need, so goes the argument, is less debt and more equity. I agree with this argument only if it is used in a precise but restrictive way. If we mean by "more equity" less leveraged balance sheets for nonfinancial enterprises and a strong equity base for the financial ones (specifically banks), this would certainly reduce the vulnerability of the corporate and banking sectors to financial shocks, notably to sudden increases in interest rates. By the same token, capital inflows in the form of direct investment also play a beneficial role—not simply because they directly contribute to higher growth, but because they also enhance the resistance of industry to shocks. This clearly applies to greenfield investments undertaken by large and wealthy foreign corporations, but it also pertains to equity investments in existing enterprises, on the grounds that such investments are made in a long-term perspective. The holders of these investments are very different animals from activist portfolio managers.

But "more equity" can mean a number of other developments as well. Consider a situation in which (a) an emerging market country has managed to create and run a large, liquid, and transparent equity market; (b) the domestic household sector has accumulated directly or through institutional investors (pension funds, say) substantial financial wealth invested in this market; (c) yet at the same time foreign investors, including a group of activist portfolio managers, own a high proportion of the country's stock market capitalisation. This would appear to be close to an ideal situation: an emerging market graduating to the position of active participant in financial globalisation. But would it really be so wonderful?

One evident advantage of such a situation would be that the domestic corporate sector would have direct access to a wide variety of financial instruments and could strengthen its own equity base. Another arguable advantage would be that equity prices could more actively play their role of leading indicators which signalled trouble ahead, thereby giving advanced warning to the government and to market participants. We saw, for instance, that in several Asian countries equity prices peaked far ahead of the eruption of the crisis (although the warning seems to have escaped the attention of most governments as well as foreign lenders). But we must also recognise that this early warning capacity of stock markets is far from being general. A third, strong argument is the one already mentioned (see Chapter 3), namely, that equity investors in general, and large investment funds from developed countries in particular, are supposed to be responsible adults who can take major losses in the event of a stock market crash—and thereby *not* act as major participants in the contagion process.

Counterarguments, however, abound. As recent experience has

shown in both Asia and Russia, equity investors from developed countries have indeed been able to absorb substantial losses without going bust, and they have therefore not been agents of contagion, at least not on a large scale, to the equity markets of developed countries. On the other hand, they did act as agents of contagion for local equity markets. Consider now the position of households in the emerging market which invested heavily in their own stock market and have lost a substantial proportion of their financial wealth in the process. We worry about the potential impact of a Wall Street meltdown on consumer spending in the United States—but what could happen to a country where real income is a fraction of that of American citizens? And what could be the impact on the newly acquired confidence in the successful working of a capitalist market economy? The point I am making here is that while in a technical sense a crisis in the form of a stock market meltdown is different from a debt crisis in which institutions and banks go bust (with all the implications for the payment and settlement systems), both the short- and the long-term effects in a poor country could still be devastating.

Improving Information

Common sense suggests that the provision of broader, more accurate, and more speedily available information should be an essential ingredient of crisis-prevention policies. This would allow lenders and investors to assess more carefully the risks associated with their portfolio management decisions and, one would hope, moderate their active participation in generating unsustainable debt or asset price bubbles. By the same token, it would also help them to adopt a more discerning attitude when it came to decisions which could lead to contagion.

Common sense is supported by contemporary finance theory, which insists that financial markets, even more than other markets, operate under conditions of information asymmetry: buyers of financial assets know less about the financial position of the issuers of such assets than the issuers themselves. From this rather safe assumption economists have built an elegant theory which explains the process of adverse selection, moral hazard, and various manifestations of financial market imperfections, such as credit rationing. The conclusion derived from both common sense and theory would then be that anything that improved the flow of information available to lenders and investors would improve the functioning of financial markets.

Formulated in this way the proposition looks uncontroversial, and I have no quarrel with it. The real questions concern practicalities: How much improvement could we expect from how much more information? What sort of information are we talking about? And what are the chances that market participants will make effective use of it? Let me take up these questions by recalling, first, recent experience.

In all four of our market crises, lenders and investors had at their disposal substantial evidence pointing to the likelihood of increased financial fragility. Well before the outbreak of the 1982–83 Latin American crisis and the current Asian crisis, the BIS banking statistics showed that countries' external bank debt was expanding at an extremely fast rate, was reaching unusually high levels, and was heavily biased towards short maturities. In the case of Asia, the heavy reliance on interbank deposits was well known.

To quote just one example, the exceptionally fast growth of Thailand's short-term external banking debt was underlined in BIS publications as early as 1994 and consistently thereafter. Neither the level of Mexico's current account deficit nor the explosive pace of domestic bank credit growth were secret; and in the months preceding the outbreak of the crisis the increasing recourse to Tesobonos financing was reasonably well documented. As for Russia, anyone who bought Russian equity and rouble-denominated Treasury bills in 1997 knew (or should have known) that tax collection was dismal, that the public-sector deficit could be limited only because public-sector salaries and pensions or suppliers of goods and services to the public sector were not paid, and that tight money, which, jointly with the pegging of the rouble, was becoming successful in slowing inflation, achieved this only by pushing the economy towards barter transactions, unpaid salaries, and stratospherically high real interest rates. It was known, at the same time, that "private" capital exports from Russia went on unabated, such that they equalled and at times exceeded imports of Western capital. What more was needed to draw the conclusion that this was a very fragile situation indeed?

Admittedly, some important pieces of information were missing. In most instances, there were no reliable data on the working of financial intermediation, for instance on the exchange-rate and maturity-transformation risks assumed by banks in Thailand, or on the unhedged exchange-rate risks assumed by Russian banks. But foreign lenders knew, within a period of four to six months, the size of interbank foreign-currency borrowing in Thailand; and even without access to reliable information on the Thai banks' balance sheets and off-balance-sheet commitments, the lenders could observe the real estate boom in Bangkok and wonder about a possible connection between the borrowings and that boom. They could also have compared the size of external interbank borrowings by banks in Thailand with the domestic credits granted by those banks. From 1990 to 1997 the percentage went up from 17 to 46. In Korea, it rose from 16 to 30. This meant that the foreign-exchange risk—borne by the banks or their borrowers—had increased considerably. Similarly, a number of large investors in Russian Treasury bills entered into substantial exchange-rate risk hedging contracts with Russian banks; they, too, could have wondered about the ability of Russian banks to withstand the effects of a rouble depreciation.

Perhaps the most important missing piece of information related to the net foreign-exchange reserve position of central banks. At the time when the IMF was called in to deal with the crisis in Thailand, the central bank's gross external reserves still amounted to $24.4 billion, but it quickly appeared that its net reserve position was close to nil as a result of its forward-exchange market intervention during the preceding six months. It is arguable that lack of information on the central bank's net external position added to the intensity of the crisis by delaying its eruption. The timely availability of such figures is therefore desirable. But I would still argue that if market participants had paid sufficient attention to publicly available information, they would have been able to detect, much earlier than they actually did, warning signals of growing financial fragility.

Why did they not do so? In Chapter 3 I gave a tentative answer to this question. On the one hand, global competition has been leading to a frantic search for profit opportunities and has contributed to herd behaviour. On the other, modern communications technology and its corollary—the modern communications culture—may have played a significant role in spreading "mono-theories" which, in turn, may be held responsible for blunting market participants' awareness of the warning signals given by available statistical information. A third factor (which I shall come back to in the following pages) has almost certainly been moral hazard, the belief entertained by lenders and investors that at the end of the day they would be bailed out by IMF-led rescue packages promoted by Western governments, mainly the United States. I find it significant that after the bailing-in experience of the early 1980s banks did not play a leading role in capital exports to Mexico during the early 1990s; but after the Mexican rescue package, in which the imprudent U.S. purchasers of Tesobonos did not lose a penny, banks from all over the world contributed massively to the process of overlending in Asia. And I have no doubt that Russia was considered by many Western investors or lenders to be too big to fail, on account of its unique geopolitical situation and because it was a major nuclear power.

The question, then, is not so much whether information should be improved—clearly it should—but how to make market participants pay more attention to publicly available information. Here are a few thoughts on this subject.

1. One way to improve information awareness would be if the IMF provided more or less explicit guidance to market participants. The most extreme involvement of the IMF (or, for that matter, any other international organisation) would be represented by an explicit risk-assessment procedure, through which the IMF would assume the credit-rating function which has been per-

formed so dismally by the private credit-rating agencies. With some justification, changes in credit ratings by these agencies (at least in the case of East Asia) have been described as the most reliable lagging indicators of an imminent crisis. Could the IMF improve on this record and, if so, should it enter into the risk-assessment business?

My answer is a clear No. It is possible, indeed likely, that the IMF can offer a better judgement on domestic policy failures or on the dangers in the build up of debt or asset price bubbles which could become unsustainable. But even the IMF can misread the significance of developments in individual countries, for the same reasons that all of us can make an incorrect judgement. And such mistakes would have far more dramatic consequences than those made by private rating agencies. Should the ratings imply excessive pessimism, they could deprive a "deserving" country of access to international capital markets. Should they be too optimistic, the IMF would be compelled to bail out creditors or investors who relied on its rating decision. Clearly, no institution endowed with lending capacity, and the duty to make use of this capacity in a crisis, should be given the task of providing credit-rating services.

But would it not be possible to argue that the involvement of the IMF in "guidance" could take on less evidently objectionable forms? Perhaps. During the late autumn of 1998, when fears about contagion hitting Brazil were widely shared, the U.S. authorities mooted the proposal of granting precautionary credit lines to countries that were pursuing the "correct" policies but were nevertheless running the risk of being driven into crisis by indiscriminate market reactions. The proposal is now (in the early months of 1999) being actively discussed by the Fund.

In light of past experience (and of my own argument about the contagion-breeding proclivity of globalisation) this would seem to be a valuable initiative. But it is not without pitfalls. To be a fully credible deterrent, any precautionary credit line would have to be almost unconditionally usable in the event of a crisis—and perhaps even be supported by a complementary commitment of at least some of the major private-sector creditors. But it is not easy to see a situation in which the IMF could, or should, undertake such a commitment. No country is ever monolithic; its policies may change over time. And what if, in case of an adverse change, the credit line has to be cancelled? Finally, on the basis of what criteria will precautionary credit lines be rationed—given the Fund's limited resources—if several countries are exposed at the same time to the risk of contagion? Alternatively, if the credit line were genuinely conditional on the country's compliance with the Fund's prescriptions, its capacity to deter speculative attacks could be impaired. This is akin to specific lender-of-last-resort actions by central banks. No wonder central banks do not commit themselves in advance to lend to specific institutions and even refrain from defining in general terms when and how they would be willing to act as lenders of last resort. They prefer to stick to a policy of "constructive ambiguity." Finding ways and means of reconciling measures to secure systemic stability with the need to avoid moral hazard will remain an unavoidably messy business.

This leads us back to the mere provision of more timely, more accurate, more detailed information on countries' financial positions. This would not by itself carry the moral hazard implied by explicit guidance. That is certainly true. But it is also arguable, on the basis of past experience, that the simple fact of disseminating more information through the IMF would be unlikely to alter lenders' and investors' herd behaviour unless the information were accompanied by qualitative comments which could be interpreted either as a warning against or an endorsement of additional risk taking. In which case we would be back to the risk of enhancing moral hazard.

2. A more promising avenue would be a shift in the practices of supervisory agencies. I make this suggestion bearing in mind my experience with the checklist devised for lending banks by Arthur Burns (see Chapter 1). On the basis of admittedly anecdotal evidence I have come to the conclusion that in all four crises financial institutions of the developed world took lending or investment decisions without paying due attention to publicly available information. I have also found evidence that while the research departments of these institutions did in many cases draw the decision makers' attention to such information, their warning somehow got lost in the process leading to lending or investment decisions or, in the worst cases, was deliberately disregarded as irrelevant. Supervisors could be entrusted with the task of ensuring that the institutions' risk-taking procedures comprise: (a) the monitoring of all relevant publicly available information, as well as, (b) the presentation of such evidence to the decision-making bodies. They should also check whether these procedures are or have been effectively implemented. Supervisors should, of course, stand clear of any involvement in the decision-making process itself. Decision makers should remain free to disregard whatever implicit or explicit advice they receive from those in charge of the monitoring exercise, but any such disregard should be explicitly motivated.

3. This takes us back to the issue of moral hazard. It is safe to assume that in a number of instances lenders or investors disregarded the warning signals provided by available statistical or other information because they believed that the capital-importing country (and, therefore, indirectly themselves) would be bailed out by international organisations and developed countries. On occasion, such beliefs are so strong that they do not need the support of past experience. But in many instances they are underpinned by such experience. Hence the crucial need to avoid, at a minimum, bailing-out practices which would imply that lenders or investors would not incur significant losses.

The Exchange-Rate Regime

We have seen that in most instances exchange-rate pegging materially contributed to the build up or the aggravation of a crisis situation. It did so in two different ways in turn. By not letting the exchange rate appreciate, pegging did not discourage "excessive" capital imports, with destabilising consequences for the country's domestic macroeconomic situation and the emergence of unsustainable debt or asset price bubbles. As a matter of fact, pegging positively encouraged capital inflows by providing a false sense of security both for foreign lenders and investors and for domestic financial institutions. When the situation changed, the defence of the peg entailed interest-rate levels which aggravated the domestic financial crisis and put a pressure on domestic demand far beyond what would have been required for external adjustment purposes—without being able to prevent excessive currency depreciation.

Many economists conclude from this that pegging should be abandoned altogether and that emerging market countries should either let their currency float freely or adopt the clear-cut alternative of a currency board regime.

I do not deny that free floating may be successful—not simply in the tautological sense of excluding the eruption of a balance-of-payments crisis but even in the more meaningful sense of enabling better management of the domestic economy whenever a country is either hit by an external shock or has to live with the consequences of earlier domestic policy failures. Sweden provided a good example in the early 1990s, as have more recently New Zealand, Australia, and (to some extent) Mexico. But I doubt that the proposition can be generalised. Rather the contrary: success is the exception not the rule. Free floating does not allow purchasing power parity to hold, certainly not in the short run (nobody pretends that it does), but not even in a medium-term perspective. With floating currencies, lasting and substantial real exchange-rate misalignments have been a frequent occurrence. Large and relatively closed economies can perhaps live with such misalignments, but even then there is a cost. It is worth remembering the potentially disruptive effects of the yen-dollar gyrations.

For small or very open economies the costs can be substantial. A sizeable and lasting real appreciation of the currencies of these economies is likely to create current account deficits that are very large in relation to GDP, so large, indeed, that they may well end up creating an unsustainable net external debt position. Once this is recognised by the markets (and we have seen that they usually take a long time to reach such a conclusion), capital will start flowing out and the exchange rate will tend to collapse to a level that is well below any conceivable equilibrium rate. In a small, wide-open economy it would require an exceptional degree of political stability and policy-making skills, not to mention a resilient system of financial intermediation, to avoid the inflation-inducing effects of such a depreciation. The vicious circle of higher inflation leading to further depreciation can be broken only by accepting ex ante (rather than as the result of deep recession and mass unemployment) a drop in real wages. There are not many countries capable of breaking out of such a bind in time to avoid accelerating inflation. The apparently strange conclusion is that genuine free floating may lead to the same disaster scenario as rigid pegging.

The extreme alternative of a currency board arrangement is also open to criticism. The choice of the reference currency is crucial: Estonia may have made the right choice in adopting the deutsche mark or Argentina the U.S. dollar, but what should Asian countries do, torn as they are between the yen and the dollar? Even more important, the successful operation of a currency board requires, not surprisingly, the same strengths as living with freely floating exchange rates: political stability, a strongly capitalised and well-managed domestic banking system, and flexible labour markets. Such a combination of virtues is rare.

It is for such reasons that I have reluctantly come to two conclusions, which are neither tidy nor elegant and which will certainly draw fire from most professional economists. The first is in addition not very original: countries, especially but not exclusively emerging market countries, differ from one another; as a result, they should not be expected to adopt identical exchange-rate regimes. The second conclusion relates to the options of exchange-rate regimes from which countries can pick. We should not exclude a priori the use of free floating or a currency board; but I would suggest that serious consideration should be given to intermediate solutions as well.

But what kind of intermediate exchange-rate arrangements? The choice will have to be made in light of several criteria. First, the arrangement should allow the exchange rate to respond to sharp, unpredictable capital in- or outflows and therefore relieve monetary policy from the burden of adopting a stance which would be in clear conflict with the requirements of domestic balance. This would require a high degree of flexibility. Second, the arrangement should also allow exchange-rate adjustment to take place in line with evolving "fundamentals"—most important, with inflation differentials. This also argues in favour of flexibility, but of the preventive rather than reactive kind. Third, however, the exchange-rate arrangement should help stabilise market expectations by providing them with an anchor—this, indeed, is the main justification for pegging.

Reconciling these three objectives may in some instances be impossible, and countries will have to accept either clean floating or a currency board type of arrangement. But reconciliation, while never easy, may pay off in other cases. Take these three criteria in the reverse order. Anchoring expectations may be helped by the establishment of a central rate defined, according to circumstances, in terms of a dominant and well-managed currency or basket of currencies. Adjustment to actual or targeted inflation differentials may be handled by resorting to a crawling peg arrangement. Flexibility to accommodate sudden shifts in capital flows can be provided by a relatively wide band around the central rate. Finally, monetary authorities may want to retain their capacity to "surprise" the market through intramarginal intervention—but they would be well advised to use this capacity sparingly.

The combination of these elements will have to be made in accordance with a number of features of the country's economy. Here are some of the key features: macroeconomic imbalance, current inflation and factors governing inflationary expectations (among which recent inflationary experiences should rank high), the degree of liberalisation of the country's capital account, the degree of its current account integration into the area whose currency serves as the reference currency, and how close the country might be to joining a monetary union.

Liberalisation of Capital Flows

Given the unquestionable contribution of short-term capital inflows to the build up of unsustainable external debt levels, a consensus is now taking hold that short-term capital inflows should be the last to be liberalised and, what is more, that they should be liberalised only after the receiving country has acquired the ability to absorb such inflows in an orderly way, without creating internal imbalances of various kinds. The proposition deserves closer inspection.

The main argument about the proper sequencing—liberalisation after the establishment of an appropriate domestic institutional framework—is surely correct, but its implications for the timing of liberalisation should not be ignored. What are the preconditions that allow a country to absorb short-term capital inflows in an orderly way? Here are a few of them. First, monetary authorities should be able to sterilise, at least in part, the money-creating impact of capital flows. This requires, among other things, a large, deep, and well-functioning domestic money market, a sophisticated set of monetary policy instruments, the ability of the central bank to cope with the valuation and income problems arising when it replaces assets denominated in domestic currency by foreign-exchange reserves in its balance sheet, and, last but not least, a great deal of skill.

Second, consider the role of domestic financial intermediation. If the capital inflow takes the form of, say, interbank deposits, domestic banks should be able to manage the resulting increase in their balance sheet without taking on undue risks of the kind accepted by banks in Thailand. This requires effective risk management and strong supervisory structures. If the inflow means the acquisition of domestic equity by foreigners, the local stock market should be liquid and resilient enough to avoid sharp, unsustainable increases in equity prices of the kind experienced by Russia. Third, the country's macroeconomic situation must be well under control. For a country with high inflation and a gaping public-sector borrowing requirement, purchases of Treasury bills by foreigners are a recipe for disaster, as the Russians have now learned. The conclusion is that satisfying all these preconditions (as well as certain others) requires time, which in the best cases will have to be counted in years if not decades. It is worth bearing in mind that a number of Western European countries achieved the full liberalisation of their capital accounts only during the early 1990s, that is, in some cases twenty to thirty years after the liberalisation of their current account transactions.

Yet at the same time we all would probably agree that foreign direct investment in emerging markets should be encouraged. But if foreign ownership of industrial corporations becomes large, it will become technically difficult to control capital movements which flow through intracompany accounts. And these difficulties will increase exponentially if foreign ownership becomes dominant in financial services and, in particular, banks. All in all, the greater the integration of an emerging market country into global markets, through current account transactions, long-term capital flows, and foreign direct investment, the less efficient will become the control mechanism on short-term capital inflows or outflows.

This does not mean, however, that rearguard action should be regarded as useless. It can, indeed, effectively delay the moment when the gates are fully opened to short-term capital inflows—even if it appears that not all capital inflows can be prevented in this way.

To begin with, countries should avoid encouraging capital imports in search of short-term gains. The classic example of what not to do is the encouragement given to foreigners by Russian authorities to buy rouble-denominated Treasury bills. Another earlier case was the deliberate selling of Tesobonos to foreign institutions by the Mexican authorities. The setting-up of the international banking facility by Thailand also falls into this category, although the motivation behind it does not appear to have been the attraction of short-term foreign money into Thailand.

More positively, prudential rules can be imposed on domestic financial intermediaries, such as the prohibition of excessive maturity transformation or of taking on unhedged foreign-exchange positions, which would discourage short-term interbank borrowing in foreign currency. Note, however, that it would not be easy to find prudential regulations which would discourage the inflow of short-term portfolio investment.

A more activist approach would consist of implementing measures that cannot be classified as prudential but could still be considered market-friendly. This could be applied even to portfolio investments. For instance, foreign buyers of domestic securities would have to put up interest-bearing deposits—but would lose part of the accumulated interest and of the deposits if they decided to sell these securities before a certain time. They would have the freedom to sell but at a cost. Any such scheme would require a well-functioning and well-controlled enforcing mechanism. The basic principle, which could be applied in a variety of ways, is the freedom to buy or sell, at a price, which would decline over the time that the foreign investor holds the asset and becomes nil after, say, six to twelve months.

Finally, in order to put a brake on short-term capital inflows, prudential rules could be imposed on foreign investors or lenders. The idea put forward above, namely, that supervisors should ensure that decision makers are aware of the existing information on debtor countries, falls, in a sense, into this category, although it would have an effect on all investments. More specifically, capital requirements could be raised on interbank lending on the grounds that "exuberant" interbank operations have played a significant role in the build up of unsustainable debt levels.

Enhancing the Resilience of Financial Markets and Intermediaries in Developed Countries

In light of what was said at the end of Chapter 3, enhancing the resilience of financial markets and intermediaries in developed countries should be regarded as one of the most important, perhaps *the* most important, component of crisis-prevention policies. Enhancing resilience to crisis manifestations serves two purposes simultaneously: it minimises the chances that an emerging market crisis will have a large-scale destabilising impact on the financial system of the developed world, and it avoids a situation in which homemade financial fragility in developed countries (essentially, asset price bubbles in the equity and debt markets and the erosion of risk premiums) coincides with an emerging market crisis. The risk of contagion is almost certainly magnified when bubbles prevail in Western markets; hence, in a sense, these two objectives may well boil down to one, the major exception being an emerging market crisis of such dimensions that it could cause by itself the destabilisation of even relatively well-balanced Western financial markets and intermediaries.

Insisting on the need to enhance the resilience of financial intermediation in the developed world to crisis manifestation should not be regarded as a purely selfish exercise, although it is that too. But maintaining the integrity of Western markets and institutions is also in the evident interest of developing countries. As I shall argue in the next chapter, the efficient and equitable handling of an emerging market crisis requires that Western institutions agree to stabilise their claims on the crisis-stricken country. The chances of achieving this are radically reduced if these institutions are themselves compelled to undertake a generalised policy of retrenchment. And in a longer perspective, the balanced growth of the world economy presupposes transfers of real resources to emerging markets, which will not happen without net capital flows from developed to developing countries. Fragile Western institutions will not provide the vehicle for such flows.

The trouble is that if the objective of enhancing the resilience of Western markets and institutions is well defined, the means of achieving it are far from obvious. Be that as it may, I cannot avoid raising some cumbersome issues and attempting to give tentative answers to them. The first two relate to the functioning of markets; the others to that of financial intermediaries.

First let us consider the role and responsibility of monetary policy in preventing the emergence, and handling the bursting, of financial (and perhaps also real) asset price bubbles. The view prevalent among central bankers has so far been that although they should not ignore the potential dangers implied by asset price bubbles in shaping their monetary policy decisions, central bankers should refrain from explicitly targeting asset price stability. To put it bluntly, they can voice concern about the appearance of a bubble but should not raise interest rates—unless the bubble coincides with the perceived danger of accelerating inflation as measured by the price of goods and services. Any such perception could arise either because of a potential wealth effect of rising asset prices on consumption or investment or because the bubble would coincide with the accelerating growth of the money supply.

Two main arguments seem to underpin this position. One concerns substance. If monetary policy manages to ensure the current and prospective stability of the CPI, it will by the same token substantially reduce the risk of asset price bubbles. The word "prospective" may be seen as implying that the growth of monetary aggregates is kept under control. The other argument concerns both substance and practicalities. Asset prices move up and down; the CPI is unlikely to fall by much. Moreover, the stability of the CPI can be defined. Some would define it as the rate of price increase falling between, say, 0 and 2 percent; others would perhaps argue that the range of stability should lie between 1 and 3 percent. In any event, prospective price movements above or below this range should trigger monetary tightening or relaxation. But what is the range of stability of equity prices? In the absence of a sensible reference zone, monetary policy could become entirely judgemental. It might overreact in either direction.

Neither of these arguments receives unqualified support from recent history. The Japanese equity and real estate bubbles of the late 1980s—which bear a major responsibility for Japan's current problems—developed at a time of CPI stability. Wall Street's "irrational exuberance" demonstrated a remarkable vitality during a period of gently declining inflation. The same happened, after a time lag, in Europe. None of these developments can be explained (as they could in East Asia or Mexico) by unwise exchange-rate pegging policies. We are driven to arguments which point either to rigidities in the real economy and retail price formation (Japan) or to the combined impact of some radical, structural shifts in labour market behaviour, productivity growth, and income distribution. But it seems to me arguable that the relatively fast growth of broad money may have played at least an accommodating role in asset price increases.

Questions can also be raised about the validity of the second argument, especially in light of the U.S. experience. During the course of the stock market boom, the chairman of the Federal Reserve Board expressed his concern about the market's seemingly irrational exuberance. The Fed's action was, however, limited to a single 0.25 percentage point increase in the federal funds rate in March 1997, an increase that did indeed put a temporary brake on the upward trend of share prices. But from April onwards, share prices resumed their climb, almost without interruption, until the outbreak of the Russian crisis. Despite this fact—the Standard and Poor's 500 index rose between April 1997 and July 1998 by more than 50 percent—the Federal Reserve took no further action. On the other hand, after the Russian crisis, the U.S. authorities reduced the federal funds rate three times in quick succession; and, obligingly, U.S. stock prices swiftly regained their precrisis peak. One can object that this comparison is unfair: the triple rate cut was probably motivated by the expectation that the Asian crisis would have a depressing effect on the U.S. economy and by the "unusual strains" which appeared in the credit and debt markets more than by a desire to stop the decline in equity prices. But the fact is that Wall Street (and European equity markets as well) interpreted this asymmetry as a sign that the price levels reached in July were not considered a dangerous bubble by the U.S. monetary authorities and reacted correspondingly. It is arguable that markets could not have gained this impression if additional interest increases had followed the March 1997 decision—which would have been facilitated if the concern about excessive asset price increase had been given a more prominent place (or a more explicit one) in the decision-making procedures of the Federal Reserve.

I do not wish to imply that the contribution of monetary policy to the prevention of asset price bubbles should take the form of explicitly including asset price stabilisation among its targets. The point made above—that it is close to impossible to define the desirable or sustainable level of asset prices—remains, to my mind, a valid objection. But neither do I believe that central banks should continue the current practice of occasionally expressing concern about stock market exuberance without following up that expression of concern with monetary tightening, especially when the equity boom is accompanied by the erosion of risk premiums and the deterioration of the quality of credits granted by banks. Such practice leads straight into asymmetry, that is, to monetary relaxation when unusual strains accompany the bursting of the bubble that no one made significant attempts to keep from developing. Once these strains are manifest, monetary policy relaxation may prove unavoidable, especially when inflation is nowhere in sight. The relaxation could mean liquidity creation, with subsequent inflationary outcome (as it did after October 1987), or increased moral hazard. Neither of these developments will make it easier for central banks in the future to dampen excessive asset price optimism. Let me make it quite clear: my implied criticism does not concern what was done after the October 1987 crash or the triple interest rate cut by the Fed during the autumn of 1998—it is directed at what was *not* done before them.

The second issue has to do with institutional improvements which would enhance the robustness of the markets. In addressing this issue we must consider, again, what appears to be a watershed in recent developments: the Russian crisis and its surprisingly violent impact on the working of financial markets in developed countries, most importantly in the United States. To anyone who doubts that this *was* a watershed I recommend a series of recent papers by government and central bank officials. The first paper was drafted by a working party of the G-10 at the request of the Halifax meeting of the Heads of State and Government in June 1995.[1] The second was prepared by a working party comprising government and central bank officials from G-10 countries and from some emerging markets.[2] The last three papers were initiated by the so-called G-22 meeting in Washington, D.C., convened at the initiative of the U.S. authorities in April 1998 "to examine issues related to the stability of the international financial system and the effective functioning of global capital markets."[3] The first two of these reports responded to the 1994–95 Mexican crisis; the last three, broadly speaking, to the 1997–98 Asian crisis. The quality of all five papers is beyond dispute. In spite of the customary difficulties encountered by working parties in coming up with clear recommendations, these papers all managed to offer a number of recommendations on an extraordinarily wide range of issues, based, moreover, on a lucid and professionally solid analysis.

The papers make reassuring reading—except on one major point. Naturally, the recommendations are addressed to emerging markets (even if that is not spelled out explicitly in all instances and even though references are made to crisis manifestations in developed countries); this was to be expected with the Mexican and Asian experiences then taking place. It could also be regarded as normal that the philosophy underlying the papers' recommendations would be as market-friendly as were most institutional reforms undertaken in developed countries with a view to strengthening the working of their markets.

After the U.S. market's "unusual strains" in September–October, however, these recommendations make strange reading. Consider the following plea for market diversity and depth from the second of the five papers:

> The most robust financial systems possess both well-functioning money markets and efficient capital markets,

including primary and secondary markets for equities and markets for a full range of fixed income maturities. The markets are sufficiently deep, with an adequate breadth of participation, so that all but exceptionally large transactions can be executed throughout the trading day without triggering excessive price movements. Robust systems also need a variety of instruments that meet the differing needs of savers, borrowers and creditors for liquidity, marketability, length of commitment and credit and market risk. Provided that the markets for the underlying instruments are sufficiently well developed, a reliable and efficient legal system is in place and financial institutions have the necessary internal controls, the availability of financial futures and derivatives enhances the potential for managing various risks. Such an array of markets and instruments contributes importantly to financial robustness. (p. 31)

None of the markets in developed countries seems to satisfy these criteria more than that of the United States. Then how is it that the Russian crisis produced in precisely this robust market the possibility of a credit crunch, a virtual standstill in bond issues for almost a month, and, most important, the surprising rise in the illiquidity premium for off-the-run Treasury securities? How can one explain the dramatically increased demand for liquidity protection? Why did the Fed have to step in to prevent fire sales by LTCM that led to disruptions in a purportedly highly liquid, deep, and transparent bond market and that risked "triggering excessive price movements"? If such developments can take place in the model market of the world, what is the practical value of recommending that emerging markets copy this model? And how is one to evaluate the role played in this model market by a clear trend towards a market-centric system?

I feel entitled to ask these awkward questions because, as I said in the previous chapter, before the September–October developments in the United States I had been tempted myself to conclude that the robustness and resilience of the financial system of the developed world constitutes the most powerful bulwark against the possibility that crises in emerging markets will develop into a worldwide crisis. After the September–October events I am not so sure. I still believe that the sizeable increase of the equity base of our banks has acted, and will continue to act, as a bulwark: banks can absorb the direct losses incurred in emerging market investments. But what about the market? LTCM seems to have gone under, and needed to be rescued, not because of poorly assessed credit risks, but because its risk-taking decisions had been based on the expectations of a certain pattern of asset price behaviour and of adequate market liquidity—expectations which turned out to be mistaken.

The next issue concerns banking supervision. Over the past couple of years supervisors in a number of countries, the United States in particular, began to consider a fairly radical departure from the methodology underlying the Basel Committee's capital ratio requirements. They had good arguments in favour of a reform. The capital ratios had initially been conceived to protect banks against credit risk. It is far more difficult to use the same techniques to cover other banking risks, especially in a world of ongoing innovation which has provided banks with a bewildering variety of hedging devices. Banks' risk-management policies have begun to vary considerably: why penalise banks which manage their risks more efficiently with an excessive capital requirement? The Cooke ratios (capital requirements on banks' credit risks) did a good job: they steered banks towards enlarging their equity base, which had been revealed as too meagre at the time of the 1982–83 Latin American crisis. But now, it is thought, they have outlived their usefulness. So the idea has gradually gained ground of shifting the emphasis of supervisors' work towards ensuring that each bank possesses a well-conceived risk-management capability and determines its capital requirements for itself; the supervisors' job would be to assess each bank's system and to check on its implementation. Admittedly, those in favour of such reform do not argue that supervisors should accept as satisfactory the level of capital that the bank's management considers adequate. The level of capital that supervisors deem necessary to protect systemic stability will almost certainly be higher. It would seem reasonable to argue that part of the additional cost should be borne by the banks' shareholders and not simply by taxpayers financing safety net arrangements. But even with this (strong) qualification, the suggested reform would hand over the initiative to bank managements. Whatever additional capital would be imposed on each bank as a result of considerations relating to a guesstimated difference between private and social cost would be added to the capital base proposed by the bank's management.

I mentioned above that I would consider it ludicrous to apply this supervisory technique to banks in emerging markets. I am now beginning to wonder about the advisability of applying it in developed countries. Or to be more precise: it is probably necessary to assess the capital requirements needed to cover market risks on the basis of the specific risk-assessment models used by each bank—this, indeed, is what is already being done. But I would caution against applying the same method to credit risks. There has always been a basic objection to the proposal: the un-availability of enough experienced supervisors to perform this highly labour-intensive, tailor-made, and judgemental supervisory function. But the banking losses announced since mid-1998 make me wonder whether banking has reached the degree of maturity required to run a system with a strong self-regulatory component. Or to put it more kindly (and perhaps more correctly): because one of the most important features of globalisation is spectacularly increased competition, should we not think that globalisation has built a twofold bias into bank management policies, namely, in favour of both excessive risk taking and excessive minimisation of the equity base?

The reader could object to the assumption that contemporary financial theory has achieved major progress in risk-assessment and risk-management techniques and that if a bank's management seeks to maximise shareholder value in the long run, it will not pursue excessive risk-taking policies. I wish this were true, but I doubt it. For one thing, I do not believe that financial globalisation will neutralise "short-termism"; on the contrary. But more important, globalisation has led us into waters uncharted by historical experience. A world in which surprises occur more frequently requires more capital and more prudence rather than less. Should we simply rely on a bank's management to realise this and act accordingly, when the bank is under constant competitive pressure and asked to maximise shareholder value in the short run? My recommendation is that unless and until we gain a better

understanding of market behaviour during the process of globalisation, it is better to abstain from such deregulation and stick to
the clumsy, primitive, and imperfect method of mandatory minimum capital ratios on credit risks. Such capital ratios should,
moreover, be set high enough to protect against systemic risk. Perhaps the day will come when this method can be abandoned, but
the time is not yet right.

The preceding argument looks sadly anachronistic. But consider the alternative, which, I submit, would be even less appealing. It would consist, to begin with, in a first layer of self-imposed
capital requirement—at least for banks above a certain size and
degree of diversification, which could be expected to carry out
their own risk assessment. This requirement would vary from
bank to bank and would be checked and approved, and its implementation monitored, by supervisors. The likely outcome would
be that, because of their increased ability to diversify their risk exposure, the larger banks would be allowed to hold less capital in relation to their assets (or to their off-balance-sheet commitments)
than smaller banks. Supervisors would then want to add another
layer of capital, on the ground that banks' shareholders should
carry at least part of the social cost associated with protection
against systemic risk. But unless this second layer varies inversely
with the first capital requirement—something that would be hard
to justify on a priori grounds and even harder to implement—the
end result would still be that size would allow banks to economise
on capital, with the public's blessing. This would create a large incentive for banking concentration at a time when (a) systemic
risks associated with globalisation would seem to warrant less
rather than more leverage, and (b) we are seeing the emergence of

enormous global financial institutions. Where would this leave us in terms of distorted management incentives and moral hazard?

The unfolding LTCM story raises, of course, other questions as well. Should hedge funds be brought under direct supervision? Three main arguments are used to answer this question in the negative. First, minimum investments in hedge funds are so high that investors can be presumed to be sufficiently wealthy to be left unprotected. The LTCM experience destroys the validity of this argument. The fund had to be rescued not in order to protect its investors but because the integrity of the market had to be protected. As far as I can see, this problem would not have arisen—at least not on this scale—had the fund been substantially less leveraged. The second argument takes into account precisely this concern. Why not deal with excessive leverage by putting supervisory pressure on lenders—mainly banks—to hedge funds? This is an avenue which deserves to be explored, but I doubt that it will lead to the desired result. After all, banks lending to LTCM *have* been under supervision. Moreover, what if nonbanks start lending to hedge funds? It seems to me that we must address the question of the direct supervision of hedge funds. The third argument concerns the feasibility of such direct supervision. If hedge funds (or other investment funds of a similar nature) were put under supervision, they would tend to emigrate towards more hospitable countries and could still disturb, in a world of free capital movements, the functioning of developed countries' markets.

I long believed in the validity of this third argument, but I do not think we can afford to believe in it any longer. A globalised world requires global supervision. To achieve that objective will not be easy. But at a time when war criminals are being prosecuted and direct military intervention against sovereign countries is considered an acceptable option, I fail to see why we should abstain from bringing pressure upon financial safe havens if they refuse supervisory cooperation. There are sufficient means to exercise graduated pressure, ranging from trade sanctions to denial of participation in the work of international organisations. It is simply not true that this would be akin to the nineteenth century's gunboat diplomacy.

5

Crisis Management

Most of us would probably agree that the best way to handle a crisis is to prevent it from happening in the first place. I certainly share this view. But I also believe that despite all prevention measures, emerging market crises will continue to occur. Both past experience and considerations relating to the ongoing process of financial globalisation point in that direction. Hence the importance of improving our crisis-management capabilities. Hence, also, the lively, often acrimonious debate (participation in which is spreading like wildfire) on who should do what, and how, when a crisis erupts.

As I explained in the introduction, my contribution to this debate will be limited. I shall attempt, in what follows, to list those requirements for the design of optimal crisis-management policies which can be derived from the four crises reviewed in the two first chapters and from more forward-looking arguments outlined in the chapter on globalisation.

Case-by-Case Handling

The most important, but also the most challenging, requirement is that each crisis be managed in its own way. Mexico Mark II was obviously different from Latin America in 1982–83; and the difference between East Asia in 1997–98 and Mexico in 1994–95 is just as great. But between the Mexico Mark II and the Asian episodes it was at least possible to detect two trends. One was the growing institutional diversity among foreign lenders and investors. The second was a decisive shift away from sovereign borrowers (except for the precrisis Tesobonos exercise by Mexico) towards private issuers of debt. The Russian crisis did not call into question the first of these trends, but it certainly did the second: the level and maturity profile of the Russian Federation's internal and external debt was at the heart of the Russian crisis. Just as the lessons that could have been drawn from the Mexican crisis would not have been helpful for handling the East Asian situation, so the latter has produced no relevant lessons for managing the Russian crisis. And who can claim to know what sort of crisis could erupt if India or China decided to join the global financial village?

The practical challenges raised by the unavailability of a standard set of crisis responses are formidable. These challenges concern first and foremost the policy conditions attached to the provision of liquidity by the IMF. These conditions cannot be defined unless the Fund's staff is able to identify, from the beginning of the crisis, several things at once. The Fund must understand, to begin with, what part has been played by domestic policy failures or simply weaknesses, as opposed to external influences such as terms-of-trade, interest-rate, or business-cycle developments in other countries. But even a reliable identification of the problem does not mean that one can define policy conditions, except perhaps in the case of lax monetary and fiscal policies. Structural weaknesses certainly need to be addressed, but it will take years for remedies in this area to become corrective. Conversely, even if much of the blame can be put on external influences over which the government has no control, domestic policy measures might still have to be called upon to play a role in restoring confidence. But how is one to assess what measures will restore whose confidence? That of foreign investors or that of domestic market participants? Answering such questions, and dozens of more difficult ones, requires not simply wide professional experience but also an in-depth understanding of how markets, institutions, politics—and society—in the crisis-stricken country function.

As globalisation embraces regions which are more and more distant—in terms of history, political reactions, and social values—from the "core" countries of Western capitalism, this analytical task becomes ever more demanding. And to the extent that one can count on an unpredictable mix of specificities in each crisis, even a wide experience with handling crises is not an unquestionable advantage: human nature being what it is, many high-powered experts tend to fight the battles of the last war. Yet there is no way out: the profile of crisis management has to be adjusted in all its aspects to the specificities of the crisis.

Bailing-in Foreign Lenders and Investors

One of the rare common features of all four crises was the build up of an unsustainable external debt burden. Extrapolating from this, we could say that when foreign lenders or investors are part of the problem, they should also be part of the solution. There are three distinct but mutually reinforcing reasons for bailing them in in the handling of a crisis.

The first reason is ethical. The level of indebtedness is determined by the interaction of demand and supply. In varying patterns, either borrowers or lenders may play the leading role. But in any event, overindebtedness cannot arise without at least an accommodating stance by the lenders. And in many instances lenders or investors have played, and are likely to continue to play, the role of initiator. There is always a shared responsibility in accumulating an unsustainable debt burden. Hence the proposition that there should also be a shared responsibility in trying to find an appropriate crisis resolution.

The second reason could be called practical. The faster the capital outflow, the more difficult it will be to manage the crisis. The availability of official liquidity assistance is finite; the macroeconomic adjustment burden falling on the debtor country rises proportionately with the size of the (additional) financing gap created by capital outflows. This is obvious when the country in crisis is operating under exchange-rate pegging. But it also applies when capital outflows contribute to accelerating currency depreciation. Such depreciation may be an unavoidable, or even a desirable, component of crisis handling. But in any case it amounts to a real welfare loss for the country's citizens. Then there is the identification problem, as mentioned above: any orderly working-out process needs time. Hence the need to provide at least a breathing space, via a standstill agreement, for the debtor country and for those in charge of the rescue operation.

Third, in a forward-looking perspective, bailing-in is justified by the necessity of tackling the moral-hazard issue. If imprudent lenders or investors suffer no losses in a crisis situation, they will start overlending again. In addition, those who have been prudent will lose the incentive to remain so. It is obvious that crisis management without a bailing-in procedure or, even worse, with bailing-out implications, prepares the ground for future crises. Crisis management with bailing-in dispositions is an absolute precondition for successful crisis prevention.

Difficulties in Standstill Arrangements

Considering standstill arrangements as one of the central pieces of any crisis management operation is unlikely to be regarded as a controversial proposition, at least in principle. When it comes to implementation, however, the obstacles become formidable. These appear well before one gets down to the nuts and bolts of drafting legally enforceable agreements, a process that raises a family of problems of their own.

At the heart of the obstacles lies the age-old problem of free-riders. Official providers of funds for IMF-led rescue packages do not want to see their money being used to bail out private lenders or investors from developed countries. In the same way, lenders or investors who would agree to the freezing of their claims, or would perhaps even agree to bringing in new funds, would not want to see market participants who were unwilling to join in a standstill agreement benefiting from their self-restraint.

A second difficulty for the design of any bailing-in programme arises out of the virtual impossibility of knowing at the outbreak of the crisis whether the indebted country or its indebted private borrowers have run into a liquidity problem or are just insolvent. This uncertainty is the rule rather than the exception. This rule, incidentally, applies even to the micro experience of corporate borrowers within individual countries: hence the universal trend towards seeking to provide an organised breathing space for corporations with payment problems before considering bankruptcy procedures. This should allow time to assess the value of the corporation's assets and, just as important, to verify whether and how the corporation could remain a going concern. When a country faces an external debt crisis the distinction between illiquidity and insolvency becomes even more blurred. The single most important additional uncertainty arises because of unforeseeable exchange-rate and interest-rate changes, which may result both from the deepening of the crisis itself and from the choice of crisis-handling policies. This has been evident in the East Asian and Russian crises. The practical conclusion is that it is hard to know in advance whether a standstill implies simply a temporary freeze of claims or whether the situation will evolve over time into rescheduling or restructuring agreements that entail varying degrees of debt forgiveness.

A third, very practical difficulty results from the growing number and increasingly varied composition of lenders and investors. In the 1982–83 crisis, banks were practically the only institutions involved. They were also limited in numbers, could be readily identified, and held their claims for their own account. They could be drawn into organised discussions with the IMF and among themselves within a matter of days. Even with such a favorable situation for consensus, obtaining an agreement on the standstill and, at a later stage, on the provision of fresh money was not an easy matter. It required imaginative leadership, cooperation with key national authorities, and peer pressure within the banking community. But it could be done, and was in fact done, without running into unsolvable free-rider problems, at any rate on a large scale. The cooperative approach even stretched over into the mid-1980s when restructuring was beginning to comprise elements of debt forgiveness. In today's world, the number of lenders or investors has grown out of proportion to the situation prevailing in 1982–83. The number of participating banks has increased. Banks have been joined by a wide range of institutional investors. Bonds have ended up in a number of retail portfolios. How can we organise such diverse, and unidentifiable, groups of lenders and investors in a way that would allow a constructive discussion with the IMF? And how can it be done swiftly?

Last but not least, a specific problem may arise if and when the IMF puts together an emergency credit package in favour of a country which is not yet in (open) crisis but is threatened by contagion. It was arguable in November 1998 that Brazil was in such a situation. The country's foreign-exchange reserves were still large and the exchange rate remained pegged to the U.S. dollar, but at the cost of steady, substantial reserve losses. Brazil was considered the next victim of contagion; at the same time, it was argued—quite rightly in my view—that even though the country ran far too large a fiscal deficit and also probably too large a current account deficit, it was silly to compare its situation to Russia's. Assuming that Brazil accepted a programme of fiscal restraint, it deserved to receive large standby credit. The IMF did indeed put together a $41 billion package, in the hope of staving off an open crisis. At the time of writing (early 1999) we know that this initiative failed to prevent the collapse of the real. Capital exports are the culprit. I do not know whether the responsibility lies with Brazilian residents or with the decision of foreign lenders and investors to withdraw their funds. But we do know one thing: although there appears to have been some sort of consensus among the leading banks on maintaining their interbank lines vis-à-vis Brazilian banks, there was not even an attempt to secure a formal standstill agreement. One of the arguments against considering any such agreement was that the mere airing of an idea of this kind would revive the memories of 1980s-style restructuring and *trigger* accelerated capital outflows. The gist of the argument was that bailing-in could perhaps be justified in a crisis but was not justified in handling a precrisis situation. Only time will tell whether this was a valid argument.

These difficulties, especially in combination, appear formidable. Yet success or failure in crisis handling will largely be conditioned by success or failure in putting in place effective standstill agreements. Without offering a detailed recommendation, for which I feel neither competent nor imaginative enough, here are a few thoughts on how we could deal with some of these difficulties.

The first point I am tempted to make is a negative one. Trying to design formal procedures, inspired for instance by Chapter 11, is not a promising avenue. This is a pity. It would be nice if it could be done, but I see no realistic chance of negotiating an internationally agreed-upon, binding legal framework that even remotely approached Chapter 11 procedures. Our legal systems are too diverse to make this possible. In addition, given the specificities which are likely to dominate each crisis, I have doubts about the wisdom of trying to design a kind of standard bailing-in "kit."

The approach should be more pragmatic, voluntary rather than mandatory, and, as far as possible, market-friendly. Market-friendliness will have to be a matter of degree; it cannot be absolute. But what seems to me desirable is that market participants should be able to make a cost-benefit calculation between accepting a standstill and withdrawing their funds. Since it is hopeless to catch all lenders and investors through constraint, the approach should apply incentives and deterrents in such a combination that foreign lenders and investors agree to participate in sufficient numbers to make a standstill effective.

In defining any carrot-and-stick mechanism several guidelines should be kept in mind. The first is that this mechanism should be tied to an IMF programme. Voluntary participation in a standstill arrangement should entail privileges—such as, for instance, access to foreign exchange provided by the Fund, according to carefully defined modalities. Second, the rewards for voluntary participation in such an organised standstill should be high enough to ensure adequate participation but at the same time should not be so generous as to significantly enhance the risk of moral hazard for the future. Third, nonparticipants should be able to withdraw their funds—otherwise we would find ourselves in a situation of unilateral moratorium or of capital export controls—but at a price, which should be, wherever possible, a market price. At the same time, this price should be stiff enough to discourage nonparticipation.

Reconciling these various objectives cannot be done in the abstract. The task will have to be adjusted to the specific requirements of each crisis. Let me illustrate this with two examples. Consider a situation in which a substantial proportion of foreign claims is denominated in domestic currency. Holders of such claims who would be willing to enter into a standstill arrangement could be offered an exchange-rate guarantee. They would be given the possibility of purchasing foreign currency, when the standstill expires, at an exchange rate which would be somewhere between the precrisis rate and the—probably sharply depreciated—current exchange rate. Nonparticipants would not be prevented from withdrawing through administrative controls, but they would have to sell their claims and buy foreign currency at market price, thereby incurring a potentially high double loss. Determining the appropriate guaranteed exchange rate is, of course, the most difficult decision. It will also not be easy to determine who the guarantor should be, particularly when the foreign claims are not on the public authorities of the crisis-stricken country but on private market participants. In the latter case, and when the claims take the form of debt obligations, debt-for-equity swaps could be envisaged as potential sweeteners.

The chances of finding genuinely market-friendly solutions are much slimmer when foreign claims are denominated in foreign currency. In this much more frequent case, crisis managers can have no recourse to the instrument of a guaranteed exchange rate. The choice for the foreign creditor is whether, by delaying the repayment of his claim, he can hope for a better deal at some time in the future. The trouble is that, whereas in the previous example the consequence of nonparticipation could be assessed by referring to a market price (the depreciated exchange rate and the—probably very low—price at which the asset could be sold in the domestic market), no such reference exists in this case. Nonparticipation would imply no repayment at all, or repayment of just X percent of the claim. And unless a negotiated settlement is reached on this percentage, the nonparticipant would in fact be facing a unilateral default or capital export controls—an option that is far from a market-friendly opting-out possibility. This situation would open the door to litigation, while in the former case the debtors could argue, perhaps somewhat disingenuously, that it is just bad luck that nonparticipating creditors have to be paid at a sharply depreciated market price.

The practical conclusion in this case is that any successful standstill arrangement requires negotiation on virtually all aspects. Creditors will have to know what degree of assurance they can get, and from whom, that at the termination of the standstill they will be repaid. They will want to know whether they run the risk of having to extend the standstill beyond the initially agreed date and, even more important, whether they will be drawn into a process of restructuring which would contain elements of debt forgiveness. And, naturally, they will want to know what the alternative of nonparticipation would entail.

Such negotiation cannot be left to the debtors and creditors. Leadership will have to be assumed by the IMF, as has been done so far in most instances. Only the IMF can enhance the credibility of any commitment by the debtors to repay the creditors on time. Only an IMF-devised set of policy commitments entered into by the debtor country's government can reduce the probability that illiquidity will turn into insolvency, with the unavoidable consequence of debt forgiveness. In turn, the IMF itself will be unable to put in place a rational financing package and gain the agreement of the debtor country's government to implement adjustment policies unless it can count on the stabilisation of the greater part of the claims of foreign lenders and investors.

This boils down to saying that speedy, efficient, and yet (relatively) market-friendly bailing-in procedures are hard to put in place when they concern lenders and investors who hold claims denominated in foreign currency. The practical conclusion is that ways should be sought to make bailing-in possible in a crisis situation before the crisis erupts—specifically, at the time when the presumably volatile short-term capital flows into the country. This puts the burden on preventive measures of the kind discussed in the previous chapter. I mentioned there the possibility of taxing withdrawals of investments before a pre-agreed date. This may not be a sufficient deterrent in the case of a violent crisis. Would it not be possible to obtain the advance agreement of foreign lenders or investors on a standstill if and when this was requested by the country's authorities—preferably with IMF approval? Any such agreement would, of course, entail a price for the borrower, but this would not necessarily be a bad outcome. This avenue seems worth exploring, although it is bound to raise innumerable legal and institutional problems.

Capital Outflow Controls

The reason for advocating negotiated market-friendly standstills, however untidy and laborious these negotiations could be, is to avoid at all costs a unilateral moratorium or, more generally, the reinstatement of controls on capital outflows. As I argued in the previous chapter, keeping the inflow of short-term capital well under control as long as possible is a desirable policy objective, even though its implementation may not be easy. But putting the lid on capital exports by foreigners, once capital movements have been liberalised, is quite another story. For one thing, the efficiency of such a policy is likely to be blunted. This much could, of course, also be said of the crisis-prevention prescription of not liberalising short-term capital inflows. But more important, backtracking on the liberalisation of capital outflows would go against the obvious long-term interests of the debtor country itself. If emerging market countries ever want to develop, they have to run current account deficits across the cycles, and these deficits will have to be financed by capital inflows, of which the best variety are spontaneous long-term capital inflows, basically, direct investment. The surest way of discouraging such capital inflows is to raise uncertainty about the possibility of getting out of the recipient country. Whatever formal guarantees are given regarding the repatriation of profits and the principal of direct investment will receive little credibility if they are provided by a country that suspends or abolishes the freedom of capital exports, even if the action applies only to, say, portfolio investment.

I have to raise at this point a major issue which has rarely been debated publicly. It concerns the outflow of domestic capital either before the open crisis or during it. In various amounts and at various times such outflows created problems either for crisis prevention or for crisis handling, or indeed for both, in all four crises discussed in this book. There are two weighty arguments in favour of bailing-in domestic market participants in the crisis-handling process. One is the same practical argument used in favour of active participation by foreign lenders and investors in standstill arrangements: the order of magnitude of the financing gap may well become unmanageably large with persistent domestic capital outflows. The other is of an ethical nature: it would be hard to justify the IMF's setting up financing packages to enable the continuation of the outflow of private capital from domestic sources.

But how can these capital outflows be brought under control? For obvious reasons, standstill negotiations of the kind advocated in the case of foreign lenders and investors are out of the question. This leaves two possibilities. One is restoring, or creating, confidence among domestic market participants. This, of course, is one of the main objectives of all IMF-inspired (or imposed) policy packages. The trouble is that in a number of instances domestic market participants will be even more difficult to persuade than foreign investors to revise their views on the chances of achieving internal and external stability or of improving yield prospects on domestic investment in comparison with returns on external investment. Russia provides perhaps an extreme example in this respect, but similar situations may well arise in other countries as well. This leaves the second possibility, that is, capital outflow controls. Once an open crisis sets in, the reimposition of such controls on domestic residents' capital outflows may become unavoidable yet turn out to be relatively inefficient. Hence the importance of not liberalising such capital outflows prematurely. This is an additional argument in favour of setting aside the ill-conceived initiative of incorporating the general principle of capital account liberalisation into the Articles of Agreement of the IMF until the time is right.

Policy Reactions in Developed Countries

Crisis management will entail in virtually all scenarios policy actions that lead to the improvement of the current account position of the country in crisis. For a country with a large current account deficit, such an improvement will be an explicit policy target; for a country with no clear current account problem it will be the more or less unavoidable by-product of crisis-fighting macroeconomic policies. Many of us may dislike the sight of a developing country undertaking an outward real resource transfer on a large scale. Most of us would prefer, in any event, such a transfer to be achieved through expenditure switching rather than expenditure cutting. But it is unthinkable that an unsustainable external debt position could be handled in practice without a policy mix that will result in a significant decline of domestic absorption, at least in the short run. In 1996 five East Asian countries—Indonesia, Korea, Malaysia, the Philippines, and Thailand—ran a current account deficit of $54 billion. It is estimated that in 1998 their current account surplus has come close to $60 billion. This is a monumental shift of $114 billion. It is conceivable that a combination of better management and better luck could have limited the size of the shift, but it would not have been eliminated.

How will such shifts be accommodated by the rest of the world? The way this is done is of crucial importance both for the world economy and for the countries in crisis. The process will either alleviate or aggravate their crisis. It will either accelerate or defuse the process of contagion. When the number of countries hit by the crisis is large, and when the world economy is far from running at full capacity, the response from the developed countries should be twofold. On the one hand, they should keep their market open for imports from the crisis-stricken countries. They should resist the temptation of invoking antidumping clauses. On the other hand, they should implement policies stimulating their domestic demand.

At the time of writing (early 1999), we are clearly in such a situation. More than one-third of the world economy is in recession. Inflation is under firm control in virtually all developed countries. The current account shifts in the countries hit by the crisis should be accommodated by growing domestic absorption in the developed world—that is, in the developed world as a whole. For we have to face up to the fact that the developed world is not a homogeneous entity. The United States has for years played the role of importer of last resort—with the result that it has built up a large and quickly expanding net external debtor position.

I do not believe that this is a sustainable pattern of development in the long run—not even for a country and a currency regarded at present as exceptionally attractive. In a financially globalised world, shifts in portfolio preferences may entail exchange-rate adjustments of truly disruptive size and duration. We would be well advised to remember the not-so-ancient story of the 1980s: the effective appreciation of the dollar by 40 percent between the end of 1980 and March 1985 was more than wiped out within the next three years. This implied that between March 1985 and early 1988 both the nominal and the real exchange rates of the deutsche mark and the yen vis-à-vis the dollar more than doubled.[1] History may, or may not, repeat itself, but it is in everybody's interest to minimise the risk of such an increase happening again. Hence the recommendation that priority be given to policies stimulating a vigorous domestic recovery in Japan and underpinning the growth of domestic demand in Europe. This could significantly ease the adjustment burden of the debtor countries and would go a long way towards containing contagion. In the long run, of course, developed countries should be net exporters of real resources to the developing world. But not in the current situation.

Conclusion

Financial fragility or, more precisely, periods of financial exuberance followed by episodes of financial distress have been integral to the working of market economies since time immemorial. Bubbles in asset prices have rarely deflated slowly: soft landings have been the exception, sharp price declines the rule. Similarly, only on rare occasions has excessive indebtedness of firms or governments been absorbed gently; more frequently the indebtedness has led to outright financial crises, with severe implications for the real economy.

The four major emerging market crises discussed in this book can be regarded as a continuation of this historical pattern. They seem to have confirmed historical continuity in another respect as well. Whereas in all four instances the manifestations of financial fragility have been aggravated by specific factors, they cannot be explained exclusively, or even primarily, by the play of such factors. Macroeconomic mismanagement in the countries concerned (or worldwide), dysfunctional financial intermediation, lack of timely information (or of its appropriate use), inadequate banking and financial market supervision, mishandled or ill-timed capital account liberalisation and domestic deregulation, inappropriate exchange-rate regimes or policies, unexpected political shocks: each of these has played at times, and in varying combinations, a significant role in aggravating the financial crises and their impact on the real economy. But they do not tell the whole story. In all four crises (just as, I would venture to say, in earlier crises) these aggravating forces added their disruptive influence to that resulting from the build up of excessive levels of short-term indebtedness by governments or the private sector and, more often than not, from the accompanying development of asset price bubbles.

These basic developments could not have taken place without the exuberant—one might also say imprudent or even reckless—behaviour of purchasers of financial assets. Without such behaviour, excessive leverage could not have developed, nor would it have been possible for equity and real estate prices to reach unsustainable levels. In a sense this is a self-evident observation. Asset price bubbles will not occur unless purchasers of assets are ready to bid up prices; and debt accumulation requires that the willing debtor meet a willing creditor (or vice versa). There can be no overborrowing without overlending.

But the story of all four crises suggests that lenders and investors from the developed world played more than just an accommodating role: in many instances they did not limit themselves to responding to the financing or borrowing requests emanating from the governments and the private sector of the emerging market countries. It is unquestionable that before the 1982–83 crisis a borrowers' market developed in international bank lending from at least 1976–77 onwards. That capital inflows were the driving force behind precrisis developments in Mexico could be seen in the upward pressure on Mexico's currency until the early spring of 1994. East Asian borrowers benefitted from the erosion of risk premiums on emerging country debt until the outbreak of the Thai crisis, and some of them had to put up with sizeable upward pressure on their currencies until early 1997. As for Russia, the explosive capital inflow during 1997 was motivated at least as much by Western banks' and institutional investors' active search for exceptional profit opportunities as by the Russian authorities' endeavours (encouraged by some weighty Western advisers) to finance their budget deficit by selling rouble-denominated Treasury bills or bonds to foreign investors. Lenders or investors from developed countries may have been spurred to participate in these phases of overoptimism by different forces or for varying reasons; they may have had a number of excuses (say, in East Asia) or very few (in Russia); but in the end these periods of euphoria were at the heart of the process which led to the trouble. This conclusion does not seem to fall far from what many economic historians and business-cycle economists used to say in the not-so-distant past.

The question, then, arises of whether this broad conclusion should be qualified, and how, when one takes into account the fact of financial globalisation. Did globalisation aggravate the four crises? And, looking ahead, is it likely to lead to more or less financial fragility?

These are ambitious questions to which I cannot pretend to have given more than tentative answers—in some crucial instances, simply by raising other questions. The single most important difficulty lies in the fact that we do not yet live in a genuinely globalised financial world. We have been moving in that direction, but we are far from having reached it; and I wonder whether we shall ever reach it. Financial globalisation is a *process* much more than a steady state. It is obviously a process in the geographical sense: it covers a growing number of countries. But it is also a process which develops a threefold interdependence: between countries or regions, between markets, and between the various components of the financial industry. It does so, moreover, in the continuously changing environment of information systems and communications technology, with successive waves of financial innovation, which are liable to affect the way interdependence evolves. New patterns of asset price behaviour may emerge; old ones may be disrupted.

Let us begin with the easy answers to my questions. There can be little doubt that the process of globalisation aggravated the crises that hit Latin America, Mexico, East Asia, and Russia. It did so, on the one hand, by (a) granting full freedom to lenders and investors located in developed countries to diversify their portfolios in the direction of emerging markets, and by (b) creating an increasingly tough competitive environment which gave them the incentive to do so. At the same time, virtually all the emerging market countries which joined the globalised world got their priorities wrong. They freed their capital account transactions and lifted a large part of administrative controls on domestic financial intermediation without establishing a solid institutional framework that would enable them to absorb large-scale capital imports in an orderly way. The disproportion in numbers did the rest. The example of Thailand deserves a special mention. During the single year of 1995 Thailand took up $36.3 billion in new banking funds. Its GDP stood at that time at about $160 billion. Finally, the threefold financial interdependence mentioned above materially contributed to contagion across countries, markets, and financial sectors.

Before turning to the impact of the process of globalisation on the markets of developed countries, I should like to make this point in order to avoid any misunderstanding: That the process of globalisation has aggravated manifestations of financial fragility in emerging markets does not mean that the cost-benefit balance of financial globalisation has been negative for them or is likely to become negative in the future. I do not believe that the East Asian countries' growth could have been what it was—and it *was* spectacular, even after allowance is made for the severity of the current recession—without liberalisation of their current account transactions and, arguably, without liberalisation of their capital account transactions and financial deregulation. Similar remarks can be made regarding the recent performance of a number of Latin American countries, although (with the exception of Chile, which was very prudent in liberalising short-term capital inflows) their growth performance has been less impressive (and much shorter) than that of the East Asian countries. The danger, however, is that if the fragility-inducing impact of financial globalisation is not attenuated, the social and political backlash might lead these countries to give up on the whole process. It is not easy to explain to those who live below the line of absolute poverty and perhaps even less to those whose rising expectations are being shattered that they should keep their eye on a trend and ignore current hardship. Alleviating the social consequences of financial crises in emerging markets should be regarded, from every conceivable angle, as a priority.

What about globalisation as it affects the developed world? Would it create a favourable environment for breeding homemade crises, that is, crises unconnected with developments in emerging markets, or would it do the opposite? Would it enable the financial system of the developed world to absorb shocks emanating from emerging markets or, on the contrary, would it tend to amplify them?

It seems arguable at first sight that for developed countries the greater part of the process of globalisation, which started sometime in the 1970s, has been completed. There are no constraints on cross-border capital movements, domestic markets have been deregulated, financial intermediaries have largely been privatised, and the institutional framework (which is lacking in emerging markets) is well established. Yet in many respects, the financial scene of developed countries is far from settled. I can see at least two areas in which globalisation is still very much a process—moreover, a process with perhaps a certain discernible direction but not a clearly foreseeable end. Developments in both areas are apt to affect financial stability in the world, but I cannot claim to know in what direction.

The first of these areas is what I would call, for want of a better expression, the institutional structure of financial intermediation. I referred several times in this book to the ongoing process of concentration in banking and financial services, mainly through mergers. This raises several questions. One concerns size. How far will concentration go? How many truly global megabanks will dominate the world? On the assumption that there will be a handful of very large global players in banking, will this create more or less stability? Optimists will argue that size allows genuine risk diversification, a large capital base capable of absorbing losses, the capacity to attract first-class managerial talent, and—who knows?—perhaps even a longer institutional memory that would enable management not to repeat past mistakes. Pessimists will point to the difficulty, which may increase with size, of maintaining adequate control over risk taking. They will also worry that decisions could be concentrated in too few hands. After all, the great advantage of a market with numerous small-sized participants is that a major error by one player will not upset the whole market. This risk is becoming greater. Very large institutions may become not only too big to fail but perhaps even too big to save. Another question has to do with the emergence of global financial-services giants that bring under the same roof traditional commercial banking (or whatever remains of it), investment banking, securities business, and even insurance. Arguments for or against could run on lines similar to those between optimists and pessimists discussed above with the added, not-unwarranted concern that the (both geographically and functionally) scattered supervisory and regulatory agencies will not be able to keep up with such developments. Third, who knows what kinds of new institutions will be created under the joint impact of technological progress and financial innovation? And how will these institutions behave? Will there be a new generation of hedge funds?

Finally, we have to keep in mind the potential influence of EMU on European banking and financial structures. The introduction of the euro has lifted a major nontariff barrier to the full realisation of the single market for banking and financial services in Europe. No one can be sure of the impact this will have on our institutional structures, but there can be little doubt that the changes will be far-reaching. And they will be happening at a time when the organisation of banking and financial-services supervision within the euro area is left more or less where it was a few years ago, that is, lagging desperately behind the challenges raised by the potentially revolutionary changes affecting European banking and financial structures. This is in stark contrast to the properly centralised decision-making procedures for the single monetary policy. The basic responsibility for regulation and supervision lies at present with national authorities, some of whom are part of (or closely tied to) the national central banks, while others are more or less independent agencies, often under government control. Moreover, although in some countries most segments of the financial industry are regulated and supervised by a single authority, in others the responsibility is scattered among different institutions. Admittedly, all these authorities cooperate among themselves under the auspices of the European Commission, and the ECB itself is expected to "contribute to the smooth conduct of policies pursued by the competent authorities relating to the prudential supervision of credit institutions and the stability of the financial system."[1] The channels of communication seem to function reasonably well. It is just barely conceivable that this cooperative framework will enable the heterogeneous group of participants to be successful, in two respects: first, in harmonising the national regulatory rules and practices so as to lift the remaining nontariff barriers to the development of an efficient single banking and financial market; and second, in reaching a consensus on the kind of financial structures that will reconcile efficiency with stability. However, given the pace at which market structures are likely to evolve, there is a genuine risk that this loose cooperative framework will be overtaken by events. Be that as it may, this risk is even greater when it comes to the crisis-handling ability of the authorities. Successful crisis handling in our globalised world requires clout, speed, and agreement on who is responsible for what initiative—precisely because the rules of crisis handling cannot, and should not, be laid down in advance. It is not obvious, to put it mildly, that the current arrangement meets these requirements.

The second area in which globalisation is still in a state of flux is the trend towards a market-centric, and away from a bank-centric, system. The U.S. financial system has become predominantly market-centric, but not that of continental Europe, at least not yet. The unusual strains which appeared in the credit and debt markets of the United States in the wake of the Russian crisis—the flight not only to quality but, more ominously, to liquidity—barely affected European markets. The 1987 stock market crash originated in the United States, not in Europe or even in the much more overvalued Japanese market. Neither of these episodes, not even the first, which I regard by far as the more disturbing, would justify even tentative conclusions in the present state of our knowledge. But they *do* warrant raising a couple of questions.

Even on the assumption (which I share) that a market-centric system is more efficient than a bank-centric one, is that system not more prone to provoke crises? But if so, can we not at least expect it to possess a self-correcting ability—an ability which derives precisely from the equilibrating function of the price movements in all markets? The answer to these questions hinges a great deal on that given to another question: What are the specificities of the price formation of financial assets in comparison with that of real assets or, indeed, with the nature of the price mechanism for goods and services? Financial asset price dynamics are harder to understand because they depend so much on liquidity and leverage. There are no convincing theories about liquidity (and even fewer about its disappearance), and there is no clear agreement on optimum leverage. If markets become illiquid, even large changes in prices may fail to clear them. And if in such a situation there are highly leveraged large-scale market participants operating in an environment of mark-to-market pricing, some of them may go bankrupt, with unpredictable consequences for the system as a whole.

When trying to assess the resilience of the globalised financial system of the developed world to crises one simple, rather obvious fact has to be kept in mind. The crucial U.S. component of our globalised system has been evolving during the past seven years in an exceptionally favourable environment. The real economy of the United States has enjoyed a long period of noninflationary boom. Long-term interest rates have been declining. With few, very short, interruptions equity prices have been rising at a pace, and to levels, that defy most forecasts. This is not an environment which provides a reliable testing ground for the resilience of a financial system. The test will come if—or I would rather say *when*—a recession sets in.

To sum up, four conclusions emerge from the first three chapters of this book. First, that the build up of excessive short-term indebtedness and the accompanying asset price bubbles were at the heart of the four crises. Second, that the exuberant behaviour of lenders and investors from the developed world played a major role in raising leverage and asset prices to levels that eventually became unsustainable, often under the influence of specific factors. Third, that the process of financial globalisation aggravated all four crises and, if left unattended, would be likely to contribute to the eruption of new crises in emerging markets. Fourth, that the jury is still out on the question of whether the process of globalisation has made the financial systems of the developed world more or less prone to manifestations of fragility.

I addressed in the last two chapters a number of issues related to policy prescriptions both in the field of crisis prevention and in that of crisis management. These policy considerations fall into two categories. Some of them aim at moderating the crisis-aggravating influence of specific factors such as macro policy mistakes, rigid exchange rates, and inadequate information (or, more precisely, the inadequate use of information). Others deal with the fundamental problem of excessive debt accumulation and related issues. In these concluding paragraphs I would like to emphasise the major themes that run through these two chapters and that motivate this second group of policy considerations. They follow directly from the analytical conclusions set out above.

The first of these themes is relevant for all players in our global financial system, be they located in emerging markets or in developed countries. However significant its contribution to efficiency gains, the process of globalisation makes our financial world a more rather than a less risky place to live in. This applies without doubt to all emerging markets which have joined, or will join, the global village. It probably also applies to developed countries: even if their financial systems prove more crisis-resistant (an outcome we cannot take for granted), they will inevitably be affected by crisis developments in emerging markets. Greater risk calls for less leverage, longer debt maturities, a stronger capital base, ample liquidity, and, most of all, risk-aware management for debtors and creditors alike. Public authorities should apply these rules, whenever applicable, to themselves and ensure that private market participants comply with them; but no amount of public action can substitute for a risk-aware management culture.

My second point is a recommendation to emerging markets. Those which have not yet liberalised their capital account operations and deregulated their domestic systems should only move in that direction gradually, *after* their domestic legal, institutional, and financial infrastructure becomes capable of dealing with the consequences of sudden large-scale capital in- and outflows. The correct sequencing of the change is essential and should be observed even if the implementation of the preconditions takes time. Those emerging markets which have already joined the global system should set as a priority the improvement of their domestic system of financial intermediation. They should also consider reinstating (preferably) market-friendly measures that allow them to keep short-term capital inflows under control, but they should refrain, for their own sake, from reestablishing controls on capital outflows. In short, active and full membership in financial globalisation should be restricted to responsible parties who are able and willing to take proper precautions. The proposal to write the requirement of capital liberalisation into the Articles of Agreement of the IMF should be quietly set aside.

As for developed countries, the key issue is to see what contribution their authorities could make to moderating the manifestations of financial euphoria among their own market participants that are likely to create trouble both for emerging markets and for themselves. Monetary authorities face a daunting challenge in this respect. They will have to avoid falling into the trap of asymmetrical policy reactions, that is, of not tightening their monetary policy stance at a time of stock market exuberance and vanishing risk premiums but being driven to relax this stance when "unusual strains" appear in their markets. Not an enviable assignment. Supervisory authorities will have to assume the no less challenging task of enforcing capital requirements on banks and other financial intermediaries when managements, which are under constant pressure to raise the return on equity as quickly as possible, argue forcefully that their own risk assessment and control systems would allow them to tolerate lower capital requirements. In addition, the IMF, other multilateral institutions, governments, and central banks will need to be aware that almost all their crisis-handling policies are bound to comprise elements that can raise the risk of moral hazard and could therefore breed renewed periods of euphoria. To make matters worse, these policies could even introduce distortions in the structure of capital flows: by granting protection—not necessarily by design but de facto—to such highly unstable capital flows as interbank deposits.

Finally, governments, central banks, and regulatory agencies will have to meet the greatest of all challenges: setting up a well-structured and efficient cooperative framework at the global level. The process of financial globalisation throws up problems of worldwide dimension which cannot be handled on an ad hoc basis. Even if all preventive measures taken by national authorities work, their sum total may turn out to be dismally inadequate for reducing the risk of a systemic crisis. And there is a genuine risk that in the case of a major crisis, national policy reactions will tend to diverge rather than converge. Establishing a cooperative framework should therefore be the major assignment for all those who are given the task of designing a new financial architecture.

Appendix A: From the BIS Annual Report on the Eve of the First Mexican Crisis

The third field in which efforts towards international co-operation should be concentrated is the international adjustment process and the financing of external imbalances. Despite the elimination of the OPEC surplus, a large number of developing countries, quite a few of the weaker industrial countries and some socialist countries continue to record substantial current-account deficits, with the counterpart surpluses being located in some of the larger industrial countries. At the same time the banks, which have hitherto contributed the lion's share to financing these deficits, are showing greater reluctance to increase their international exposure. It would be regrettable, however understandable, if the banks' growing caution, often inspired by current political tensions, were to extend too widely and too indiscriminately to whole groups of countries. In

BIS Annual Report, 1982, pp. 188–89.

the absence of active international co-operation, this could well impel too many borrowing countries to adjust too fast, with a cumulative depressive impact on the world economy. It would be ironical if this were to happen just when the world has weathered for the second time the major disequilibria born of the successive oil shocks.

This Report is in no way suggesting that all the present deficits deserve to be financed. A number of them are due to manifest errors of management which it is primarily the deficit countries' own responsibility to remedy. But corrective measures take time to implement. Moreover, there are deficits on current payments which, even more clearly, seem to warrant financing, at least on a temporary basis: where, for instance, a country has just demonstrated its determination and ability to adjust by achieving a major improvement in its trade balance, but where the effects of this are partly or wholly offset by increases in interest charges on external debt. Finally, even where the country's current account is in balance, attempts on the part of some banks to reduce their international exposure are likely to make straightforward refinancing of an external debt difficult. In many cases, external reserves are insufficient to meet the repayment of maturing external debts.

This situation underlines the fact the we are still far from having found a reasonable balance between adjustment and financing of external disequilibria or, on the financing side, a reasonable division of labour between private bank credits and official flows of funds. In an ideal world deficit countries would undertake corrective measures in a timely fashion, while international capital flows would promote investment in the capital-importing countries or help orderly domestic adjustment whenever an unsustainable external imbalance arose. They would reward rational policies rather than facilitate economic mismanagement. Gradual conditionality in the early stages of an emerging imbalance would clearly be preferable to over-generous lending initially, followed later by a sudden drying-up of external finance.

But the world is not an ideal place, and more nearly ideal adjustment policies and lending procedures will take years of learning by the policy-makers of the borrowing countries, by the lending banks and by the official institutions. At the present stage of this learning process—and bearing in mind that, given the counter-inflationary slow growth scenario in the industrial countries, drastic global adjustment elsewhere in the world would have to take the form of cutting imports—international co-operation should aim at strengthening the rôle of official financing. Selective intervention by official institutions, most of all by the IMF, constitutes at this juncture the best way of channelling adjustment efforts in the right direction and at the same time of restoring, with necessary caution, market confidence. This is a task which is perfectly within the power of international co-operation—even in a cold political climate.

Appendix B: Statement by the G-10 Central Bank Governors on International Lending, 1980

1. At their meetings in Basle on 10 March and 14 April the central-bank Governors of the Group of Ten countries and Switzerland exchanged views on the evolution during recent years, and the future prospects, of the international banking system in general, and the Euro-currency market in particular.

2. The Governors recognise the important part played by the banks in recycling large surpluses which have arisen during the last few years. They noted that international bank lending aggregates have been expanding at an annual rate of some 25 per cent. Moreover, the contribution of the external banking system to re-cycling the large OPEC surpluses that have re-emerged will lead to further substantial growth of these aggregates.

3. In view of the present volume of international bank lending

Press Communiqué, Bank for International Settlements, 15 April 1980.

and of its prospective future rôle the Governors are agreed on the importance of maintaining the soundness and stability of the international banking system and of seeking to avoid any undesirable effects either worldwide or on the conduct of policy in particular countries.

4. With these considerations in mind, the Governors have decided to strengthen regular and systematic monitoring of international banking developments, with a view to assessing their significance for the world economy, for the economies of individual countries, including particularly the operation of their domestic monetary policies, and for the soundness of the international banking system as a whole. A Standing Committee on Euromarkets will consider the international banking statistics compiled by the BIS and other relevant information and report to the Governors at least twice a year, and more frequently if developments call for it. These arrangements for closer surveillance could provide a framework for intensifying, if appropriate, co-operation on monetary policies between the countries concerned.

Notes

Chapter 1: Four Crises: An Overview

1. Except where stated otherwise, all external bank debt figures in this section are taken either from the international banking statistics published by the BIS, or from the bank's Annual Report of 13 June 1983.

2. See Martin Feldstein, Hervé de Carmoy, Koei Narusawa and Paul R. Krugman, *Restoring Growth in the Debt-Laden Third World: A Report to the Trilateral Commission.* Triangle Paper, April 1987.

3. For a masterful summary of the argument, and supporting statistical evidence, see Feldstein, de Carmoy, Narusawa and Krugman, *Restoring Growth in the Debt-Laden Third World.*

4. The dollar rose from 80 yen (March 1995) to 130 yen (December 1997).

5. In its Annual Report published on 10 June 1996 the BIS noted: "The unprecedented volume of [new bank] lending to Asia suggests that the impact of the Mexican crisis on the region was at most marginal. Apart from its sheer size, four features characterised bank credit to Asia in 1995. First, two-thirds of the total was in the form of short interbank lines. . . . This, together with sizeable trade-related loans, meant that by mid-1995 64% of the outstanding claims on the region were of less than

one year. Secondly, Thailand and Korea took up $36.3 billion and $22.3 billion of new funds respectively. By year-end, Thailand had become the largest bank debtor in the developing world."

6. BIS Annual Report, 1998, p. 146.

7. India, Indonesia, Korea, Malaysia, the Philippines, Singapore, Taiwan and Thailand. See BIS Annual Report, 1998, p. 133.

Chapter 3: Does Financial Globalisation Aggravate or Alleviate Market Problems?

1. BIS Annual Report 1998, p. 100.

2. BIS Annual Report 1998, p. 84.

3. BIS Annual Report 1998, p. 122.

4. Alan Greenspan mentioned a loss of $30 billion by U.S. investors alone (testimony before the Committee on Banking and Financial Services of the U.S. House of Representatives on 30 January 1998).

Chapter 4: Crisis Prevention

1. *The Resolution of Sovereign Liquidity Crises.* A report to the ministers and governors prepared under the auspices of the deputies, G-10, May 1996.

2. *Financial Stability in Emerging Market Economies.* Strategy for the formulation, adoption and implementation of sound principles and practices to strengthen financial systems, April 1997.

3. *Reports on the International Financial Architecture:* Report of the Working Group on Transparency and Accountability; Report of the Working Group on Strengthening Financial Systems; Report of the Working Group on International Financial Crises, October 1998.

Chapter 5: Crisis Management

1. BIS Annual Report 1988, chap. 7.

Conclusion

1. Article 105 (5) of the Maastricht Treaty.

Glossary

ADB Asian Development Bank

Band (around the exchange-rate peg) Boundary within which a country's monetary authorities allow the market value of a currency to fluctuate. *See* Exchange-market intervention; and Peg, Pegging

Basel Committee Committee of G-10 Bank supervisors meeting in Basel, Switzerland, under the auspices of the BIS. *See* BIS; Cooke ratios; G-10

BIS Bank for International Settlements, owned by the major central banks. It acts as the central banks' money-market bank and serves as a vehicle for central bank cooperation—for example, in the field of bank supervision or in monitoring financial market developments.

Borrowers' market A market situation which, as a result of active competition among lenders, is favourable to borrowers.

Bridging loan   A short-term loan granted to a borrower who is expected to receive a long-term loan and repay the lender out of the proceeds.

Chinese walls   Rules established within a financial institution to prevent the free flow of information between sections of the institution which may have conflicting interests.

Cooke ratios   Capital requirements on banks' credit risks established by the G-10 supervisors at the time when their chairman was Peter Cooke.

CPI   Consumer price index

Crawling peg   Exchange-rate arrangement for changing the peg according to predetermined rules—for example, to preserve the country's competitive position. *See* Effective-exchange rates; and Peg, pegging

Debt relief   Reduction of the burden carried by the debtor, which may take the form of partial or even total debt forgiveness, or the easing of the debt-servicing obligations.

Derivatives   Financial contracts or securities related to—"derived from"—underlying contracts or securities. For example, an interest-rate swap is an agreement between two debtors to exchange, on the basis of predetermined rules, future flows of interest payments. A debtor whose liability carries a fixed interest rate may in this way "swap" its interest payments against the variable interest commitments of his counterparty. In such a contract the payment is made to cover the difference between the two flows of interest payments. No payment is made or received on the underlying debt. *See* Notional (principal or amount)

ECB   European Central Bank, i.e., the central bank of EMU

Effective (nominal or real) exchange rates   The nominal effective exchange rate of a country is the weighted (often trade-weighted) average of bilateral exchange rates. The real effective exchange rate is a nominal effective exchange rate deflated by a weighted average of foreign prices or costs relative to the domestic ones. An increase in the real effective exchange rate indicates a deterioration in the country's competitive position, while a decline shows an improvement.

EMU   Economic and Monetary Union (in Europe)

Euro   The European currency, managed by the ECB, which came into existence on 1 January 1999.

Exchange-market intervention   Buying or selling a country's currency in the market by its monetary authority with the intention of raising or lowering its value in relation to the peg (*see* Peg, pegging). Intervention is called intramarginal when it takes place within the band (*see* Band).

Expenditure switching versus expenditure cutting   Expenditure switching occurs when a country's current account deficit is corrected in such a way (typically by devaluing the currency) that the depressing effect of a cut in domestic spending on the level of activity is offset by an increase in exports.

FDI   Foreign direct investment

G-10   The Group of Ten countries (actually eleven): Belgium, Canada, France, Germany, Italy, Japan, the Netherlands, the United Kingdom, the United States, Sweden, and Switzerland. The group was established in the early 1970s with the objective of promoting monetary cooperation among the most developed countries.

G-22   Twenty-two "systemically significant countries" whose finance ministers and central bank governors were convened to a meeting in April 1998 in Washington, D.C., at the initiative of the United States to examine issues related to the international financial system and the functioning of global capital markets.

GDP   Gross domestic product

Hedge   A financial commitment (for example, to buy or sell a financial asset) undertaken with a view of protecting the investor against adverse changes in the value of, or the income from, its investments.

Hedge funds   One of the most misleading expressions used in contemporary finance. Most hedge funds are investment funds practising a very aggressive investment policy by taking highly risky positions. However, some of them do actually hedge.

IBRD   International Bank for Reconstruction and Development (the World Bank)

Large value payments   Very large payments exchanged between banks or financial market participants.

Leverage   The multiplier effect on profits of a small change in sales or prices resulting from a balance sheet or option structure; a corporation, for example, is said to be highly leveraged when it operates with a high debt-to-equity ratio.

Liquidity   A market is said to be liquid when a seller (or buyer) of a financial asset is able to find a buyer (or seller) without significantly affecting the prevailing market price.

LTCM   Long-Term Capital Management, one of the most prestigious hedge funds, which came close to bankruptcy in September 1998 but was bailed out by a consortium of banks acting under the auspices of the Federal Reserve Bank of New York.

Marking-to-market   Valuing a portfolio or a trading position on the basis of current market prices.

Moral hazard   A concept of the insurance profession, now widely used in contemporary finance theory. The fact of being insured (say, against fire) may lead the insured person to become careless (say, by neglecting to take normal fire prevention measures). By analogy, a problem of moral hazard arises when a lender or investor acts on the assumption that it will be bailed out, directly or indirectly, by a lender-of-last-resort—the IMF, for example—if the borrower is unable to fulfill its obligations.

Netting, net settlement system   A funds-transfer system in which settlement is completed on a net basis. *See* RTGS

Notional (principal or amount)   Refers to the hypothetical amount on which a derivative contract is based. In the case of interest-rate swaps, for example, it refers to the underlying debt. *See* Derivatives

OECD   Organisation for Economic Cooperation and Development. Originally only developed, "industrial" countries were members, but more recently membership has been extended to "advanced" developing countries.

OPEC   Organisation of Petroleum Exporting Countries. The group does not include, however, a number of major oil exporters (for example, Mexico and Norway).

OTC *(contracts)*   Over-the-counter transactions, mostly in derivatives, between financial market participants. The counterparties have to agree among themselves on the specificities of each contract. Recourse to standard models is rare, as opposed to transactions carried out on organised exchanges, which are all standardised.

Peg, pegging   Fixing the value of a country's currency in relation to another currency or to a basket of currencies. Typically, however, the country's monetary authorities define a band around the peg—which can be "narrow" (say, ± 2 percent) or "wide" (± 15 percent)—within which they let the currency fluctuate. *See* Band; and Exchange-market intervention

Real resource transfer   An outward real resource transfer occurs when a country exports more goods and services than it imports. An inward real transfer refers to the opposite situation.

Rescheduling (of debt)   Agreeing on a new repayment schedule—typically, by delaying repayment.

Rollover loan   A (typically medium-term) loan carrying a short-term interest rate which is periodically readjusted to the prevailing market rate.

RTGS   A real time gross settlement system in which the settlement of payment orders takes place without netting (i.e., on an order-by-order basis) and in real time (continuously). *See* Netting, net settlement system

Securitisation   In the narrow technical sense, converting non-tradeable bank claims (e.g., real estate mortgage loans) into securities which can be sold on the market. Also used to describe the increasing share of securities in total debt flows.

SME   Small and medium-sized enterprises.

Sovereign debt   Debt owed by a state.

Standstill agreement   Agreement by which creditors agree to "stand still," i.e., not to request a debt repayment at the contractual maturity date.

Tesobonos   Dollar-indexed Mexican Treasury bills

Index